No
Bro

A Northern Bro

C000092419

"We are three Sisters"

by Blake Morrison

Cast (in order of appearance)

CHARLOTTE BRONTË	Catherine Kinsella
ANNE BRONTË	Rebecca Hutchinson
EMILY BRONTË	Sophia Di Martino
PATRICK BRONTË	Duggie Brown
DOCTOR	John Branwell
TABBY	Eileen O'Brien
CURATE	Marc Parry
BRANWELL BRONTË	Gareth Cassidy
TEACHER	Barrie Rutter
LYDIA ROBINSON	Becky Hindley

The Team

Director	Barrie Rutter
Designer	Jessica Worrall
Lighting Designer	Tim Skelly
Sound Designer	Kraig Winterbottom
Music	Conrad Nelson
Production Photographs	Nobby Clark
Production Manager	Kay Burnett
Company Stage Manager	Guy Parry
Technical Manager	Richard Walker
Deputy Stage Manager	Bryony Rutter
Wardrobe Supervisor	Hannah Blake
Education	Deborah McAndrew
Executive Director	Sue Andrews
Marketing	Lisa Baxter Arts Marketing
Press	Duncan Clarke PR

**This production was first performed on
Friday 9th September 2011 at the Viaduct Theatre, Dean Clough, Halifax**

Blake Morrison writes...

Charlotte Brontë liked to give the impression nothing of interest ever happened to her and her sisters – Haworth being a remote spot, and life at the parsonage lacking in incident. And yet the lives of the Brontës have been retold – on stage, on film, in fiction, even as ballet – as often as their novels have been adapted. That's because they raise such fascinating questions. How did three sisters come to write such groundbreaking novels? What was the chemistry between them? Why did they adopt pseudonyms? What experience, if any, did they have of being in love? How did they cope with their wayward, drug- and booze-addicted brother Branwell? How congenial was the influence of their father Patrick, whose health they constantly worried about, but who outlived them all? How feminist were they? How political in their thinking? Far from being uneventful, the lives of the Brontës are so full of psychological interest and dramatic potential that it's hard to know where to start.

For me the starting point was Chekhov, whose play *Three Sisters* explores many of the themes that preoccupied the Brontës: work, education, marriage, the role of women, the dangers of addiction, the risks of flirtation, the rival claims of country and city, the stirrings of political unrest. The parallels are no mere coincidence. According to Chekhov's biographer, Donald Rayfield, one of the books he ordered for the library of his home town, Taganrog, and which he kept for nearly a month before sending it on, was an account of the Brontës by Olga Peterson (a Russian married to an Englishman). The fact that Chekhov's dancing teacher at school was a Greek called Vrondi, and in demotic Greek (which Chekhov knew a little) Brontë and Vrondi are virtual homonyms, may have tickled his fancy still further.

The immaculate structure of Chekhov's play also attracted me. Its four acts span a period of four years, yet it feels much shorter, because it is so tight and focused. By using it as a template, I was forced to concentrate on a brief but intense phase of the Brontës' lives, involving the fallout from Branwell's affair with his employer, Mrs Robinson (a gift of a name), and the publication of Charlotte, Emily and Anne's first novels. I've allowed myself some licence with chronology. But in effect the play occupies a few weeks in early 1848, with Chartist riots brewing in the background, and the deaths of Branwell, Emily and Anne (which occurred within a period of nine months) looming ahead.

The Brontë story is usually shrouded in darkness and misery. *We are Three Sisters* tries to disperse the gloom and to highlight resilience instead. Despite the tragic events of their childhood (the deaths of their mother and of two of their sisters), Charlotte, Emily and Anne were not pathetic victims of fate, but strong-minded, independent and resourceful women. Nor was Haworth a godforsaken spot in the back of beyond: as Juliet Barker shows in her marvellous biography of the Brontës, both the industry and the intellectual life of the region were thriving. Patrick Brontë has often been stereotyped as grim and reclusive. But he used his position to campaign fiercely for better education and sanitation for the people of Haworth. Another stereotype about the Brontës is their lack of humour. But there's a playful air to some of Charlotte's letters. I wouldn't call *We are Three Sisters* a comedy, exactly, but with Chekhov's encouragement I've tried to let in a little lightness.

Chekhov's three sisters pine for 'Moscow, Moscow, Moscow'. The Brontë sisters were more ambivalent about London, but when her friend Ellen Nussey failed to be moved by a visit there, Charlotte told her off: 'Had you no feeling of intense, and ardent interest, when in St James's you saw the Palace, where so many of England's kings had held their Courts?... You should not be too much afraid of appearing country-bred. The magnificence of London... is to me almost as apocryphal as Babylon, or Nineveh, or ancient Rome.'

Wherever possible, I've tried to be true to the Brontës' thoughts and feelings. As well as drawing on Juliet Barker's biography, I've used words that appear in the novels, Charlotte's letters, and Elizabeth Gaskell's biography. Here, for example, is Gaskell's account of Charlotte telling her father about *Jane Eyre*:

'Papa, I've been writing a book.'

'Have you, my dear?'

'Yes, and I want you to read it.'

'I'm afraid it will try my eyes too much.'

'But it is not in manuscript: it is printed.'

'My dear! You've never thought of the expense it will be!...'

This episode has been imported into the play almost verbatim. So has Charlotte's account of the trip she and Anne took to London in order to reveal their identities to their publishers – 'We are three sisters' – and how betrayed Emily felt as a result.

For me, *We are Three Sisters* is a kind of homecoming. I grew up within striking distance of Haworth, in an old rectory at the top of a village and with a view out onto moors. And when the composer Howard Goodall approached me with the idea of collaborating on a musical of *Wuthering Heights* back in the 1980s, I was quick to accept. Leicester Haymarket Theatre seemed interested in staging it. But there were five musical versions of *Wuthering Heights* doing the rounds at the time, and in the end it was Tim Rice's *Heathcliff*, starring Cliff Richard, that prevailed. I thought that was the end of my relationship with the Brontës. But thanks to Susannah Clapp (who first suggested the idea a decade ago) and Barrie Rutter (who nagged me to get on with it last year), here I am involved with them again. It's good to be back.

Photo © Nobby Clark

Blake Morrison and Barrie Rutter

Notes from the Director...

The three weird sisters of *Macbeth*; Lear's three daughters; the Fates: Clotho, Lachesis and Atropos; The Gorgon sisters: Stheno, Euryale and Medusa; the three sisters from Native American agriculture: maize, squash and beans; the Furies: Tisiphone, Megara and Thalia; and the three Chekhov Sisters themselves... not to mention the Three Degrees, Diana Ross and the Supremes, the Beverley Sisters or the much trampled slopes of the Three Sisters in Glencoe and yet and yet... the three most famous sisters of all are just up the road in Haworth! Charlotte, Emily and Anne Brontë; Yorkshire lasses, authors, pioneers; three young women absorbed in an exuberant childhood and wild, imaginative games who would grow to astonish the literary, male leaseholders of nineteenth-century Britain with their publications of *Jane Eyre*, *Wuthering Heights* and *The Tenant of Wildfell Hall*.

Yorkshire-born poet and author Blake Morrison has provided his sixth play for Broadsides; Yorkshire-born self-confessed Brontë nut Jessica Worrall has designed the set and costumes; Yorkshire-born scholar and internationally recognised authority on the Brontës, Juliet Barker, has intrepidly offered comments as the fusion between Chekhov and history took shape; and then me! Yorkshire-born and leagues behind the above in Brontë knowledge, but at the helm of this production and improving my affinity and affection for the sisters with each new page and rewrite of this script.

Enjoy!

Barrie Rutter

Photo © Nobby Clark

Sophia Di Martino, Rebecca Hutchinson and Catherine Kinsella

Notes from the Designer...

As a long-term admirer of the Brontë sisters and their work, it was with a veritable air of excitement that I first became involved in working with Blake and Barrie on this new play. The excitement was easy to understand: anything that involved endless hours conjuring up images and ideas of the Brontës was hardly a difficult undertaking, but what was surprising and totally unexpected was the accompanying sense of trepidation, almost a fear, that seemed to come from a growing sense of responsibility, which I felt not only to the subjects and their work but also to the long-cherished visions that I have of them and the important role they have played in my life.

My admiration began when I first read *Jane Eyre*, a momentous event in any young girl's life, swiftly followed by my first visit to the parsonage and the waiting world of all things Brontë; that seemingly endless climb up and up the narrow lanes over the cobblestones, until finally you reach the house, perched precariously between open moor and closed graves. Strangely imposing from the outside (even without the extension built after the Brontës' occupation), I think it works more as a kind of inverted tardis, impossibly small on the inside, everything in its place, neat as a pin but scarcely enough room for a family with six children. Even after the loss of their mother and two elder sisters, it must have still felt full of life, bursting at the seams with the never-ending ideas and stories of Charlotte, Emily and Anne; it seems incredible that the whole of Haworth didn't know about them, let alone their father.

It was thinking of the three girls and that dual reality of their visible and secret lives that influenced my approach to the design. I wanted to blend the external and internal – firstly in a practical sense, merging the contained parameters of their home with the wider and wilder context of both the social and natural worlds in which it stands; but secondly, avoiding an overly literal representation of the dining room at the parsonage where most of the play takes place. Whilst veracity of period and place was vital, it also seemed important to incorporate some semblance of those now-familiar literary places the sisters brought into being in their nightly wanderings round and around the table; Wildfell Hall, Wuthering Heights, Thornfield. The solution seemed to lie in creating something both practical yet emotional, functional yet psychological.

I found the same approach suited the costumes. Whilst keeping strictly to period, it was hard to ignore the descriptions of some of their supposed literary counterparts – who can forget Jane Eyre's description of herself as 'obscure, plain and little'. The inevitable comparisons we draw from the novels is perhaps understandable given the scarcity of actual images of the family: a couple of (disputed) photographs of Charlotte, a few sketches and caricatures, and of course the famous pillar portrait of the three sisters by their brother. However badly executed, it is nevertheless something truly to thank the hapless Branwell for.

The other details I have kept are both Brontëan and Chekhovian. Emily's outdated dresses, her refusal to wear a corset and the required amount of petticoats; Patrick's large necktie worn to ward off infection, and Mrs Robinson's green dress, the colour often used by Chekhov to symbolise death or bad luck and worn by Natasha in *Three Sisters*.

I hope that this combination of fact and fiction, of reality and imagination, echoes the nature of both Blake's play and the Brontë sisters themselves.

Jessica Worrall

In the beginning...

It first hit me about ten years ago. Watching *Three Sisters* – was it at the Lyceum in Edinburgh or at the Chichester Festival Theatre? – something tugged at me: it was as if I were seeing the play in unexpected binocular vision, or sensing a shadow behind the action. The family arrangement – three gifted sisters and a revered but hopeless brother – struck me as familiar. As did their longing. And their claustrophobia.

And then I got it. Charlotte and Emily and Anne, with Branwell hovering around as an unfulfilled genius. It was the Brontës. I didn't know then, as I would have had I read more of Chekhov's letters or studied the biographies, that the Brontës were if not exactly a source, at least an influence on the playwright when he wrote *Three Sisters*. I took the echo as being yet another sign of Chekhov's extraordinary power, another empathetic leap. And I mentioned it to Blake Morrison.

Why to Blake? Well, we are friends, and I'd much admired the work he had done in bringing classical dramas to vivid Yorkshire life with Northern Broadsides. I was particularly stirred by his West Riding version of *Oedipus*, which gives Sophocles' terrifying tale a wild but homely setting and his characters a particular mental landscape, one in which a bad marriage is 'a stormy moortop of bramble and gorse'.

I wasn't proposing that the Brontës should be whisked off to Russia, nor that silver birches and samovars should be dropped on Haworth; I was simply fascinated by the correspondence between these two sets of sisters and couldn't shake off the resonance. I didn't know what to do with it, though. Nor did Blake, who was intrigued but thought the whole thing a bit 'bonkers'. We had a couple of chats about the sibling trios, the last over an un-Russian, un-Victorian coffee and cake in a Southwark café – and then we let it drop.

Until January last year, when I was making a documentary about Chekhov for Radio 3. The programme, which took off from the playwright's sense that he would be forgotten within a decade of his death, had at its centre new and lovely translations by Sasha Dugdale of scenes from *Three Sisters*: though there were no violent surprises in the vocabulary, the dialogue was restrung so that it moved to a different rhythm. Between interviews, the producer Beaty Rubens and I fell to talking about the small things that brought an adaptation to life and made it distinctive, and about the extraordinary flexibility of Chekhov's plays. Apparently infinitely prone to relocation, we agreed – looking back on Mustafa Matura's Trinidadian version. I said that I'd even once wondered whether something couldn't be made of the resemblance between the Brontës and the three sisters. It would, I muttered, be just the job for Northern Broadsides. And then we moved on to some knot in my script.

I didn't know that Barrie Rutter was not only in London that week, but in Broadcasting House, rehearsing Lenny Henry for the broadcast of *Othello*. I didn't know that Beaty would run into him, that she would not only remember my tossed-off remark but repeat it. But he was and she did. And so, a decade after our first conversation, Blake and I found ourselves in another London café talking about Haworth. It turned out, for all the bonkerishness of the project, he had kept a whole notebook about it: one that was crammed with ideas. And it turned out that he could draw on this to produce a play which evokes both the Brontës and the Prozorovs, while being particularly Morrison. Reading it (I've yet to see it) made me feel as if I was looking at the famous picture of the sisters – the one painted by Branwell from which he brushed himself out – and seeing other faces poking over their shoulders from the shadows.

I'm pleased to have had a small, voices-off part in *We are Three Sisters*.

Susannah Clapp

Susannah Clapp writes about theatre for the *Observer* and talks about it for Radio 3's *Nightwaves*. She is the author of *With Chatwin*, a portrait of Bruce Chatwin, and is writing a book about postcards.

Cast and Team

John Branwell (*Doctor*)
Theatre includes: *A Midsummer Night's Dream, The Cracked Pot, Oedipus, The Game* (Northern Broadsides); *Comic Potential* (Lyric); *The Sea* (Theatre Royal Haymarket); *The Safari Party* (New Hampstead); *Jail Diary of Albie Sachs* (Young Vic); *Way Upstream, Haunting Julia, Time and Time Again, Woman in Mind* (Stephen Joseph); *The Life of Galileo, Tom and Vic, Canterbury Tales* (Library, Manchester); *King Lear, Bouncers* (Nottingham Playhouse); *Romeo and Juliet, A View From the Bridge, The Taming of the Shrew, The Magistrate, Much Ado About Nothing, Othello, See How They Run* (Manchester Royal Exchange); *House and Garden* (Salisbury Playhouse); *Blue Remembered Hills, Comedy of Errors, The Hairy Ape, Comedians* (Octagon Theatre Bolton); *When We Are Married, The Crucible* (Leicester Haymarket); and much new work for the theatre by writers including Alan Ayckbourn, Alan Bleasdale, Peter Flannery, Henry Livings, Tim Firth, Blake Morrison, Willis Hall, Bernard Kops, Andy de la Tour and John Godber. Television includes: *Emmerdale, Coronation Street, Heartbeat, The Royal, Doctors, Midsomer Murders, Foyle's War, Dalziel and Pascoe, Swallows and Amazons, EastEnders, The Cops, Holby City.* Film includes: *Rebecca, West is West* (sequel to *East is East*).

Duggie Brown (*Patrick Brontë*)
Granada Television's series *The Comedians* established Duggie Brown as a national entertainment figure, although he was already well known throughout the UK with his successful cabaret act. In the early seventies, Duggie moved into the drama field, beginning with an appearance in the iconic Ken Loach film *Kes*. Numerous roles followed including *Another Sunday and Sweet FA, Rank and File, The Price of Coal,* for the BBC and *The Hard Word* for ITV. He was then to star in the Shelagh Delaney BBC Series *The House That Jack Built,* followed by the BBC detective series *The Enigma Files.* For Granada TV he starred in *Take My Wife* and *The Glamour Girls.* He was also the Captain of the Saturday morning children's series *The Mersey Pirate.* Duggie's other television roles include *Brookside, Coronation Street, Heartbeat, The Bill, Minder, Ellington,* the BBC Drama series *The House of Cards, Doctors, A is for Acid, Fat Friends, EastEnders,* and *Hotel Babylon* to name but a few... His other film work includes *Between Two Women* by Steven Woodcock which was released in the USA and the follow-up production entitled *The Jealous God.* His work for the theatre includes performances at Liverpool Playhouse, Nottingham Playhouse, The Little Theatre, Middlesbrough and The Grand Theatre, Leeds. Duggie also directed and starred in a brand new musical play called *Danny* which toured for six months, with him playing the part of Father O'Laughlin. Duggie has previously appeared for Northern Broadsides Theatre Company as The Fool in Shakespeare's *King Lear* and is delighted to be returning to work once again with director Barrie Rutter as Patrick Brontë in *We are Three Sisters.*

Gareth Cassidy (*Branwell Brontë*)
Theatre includes: *Heidi – A Goat's Tale* (Northern Broadsides); *Hard Times* (Library Theatre Company); *Peter Pan* (Dukes, Lancaster); *Twelfth Night* (Cottongrass Theatre Company); *In The Picture* (M6 Theatre Company); *Crying in the Chapel – The Strangeways Uprising* (Contact); *The Merchant of Venice, Hamlet* (Demi Paradise at Lancaster Castle); *A Spectre Calls* (JB Shorts); *CELL* (24:7 Theatre Festival and Library, Manchester); *The Revengers' Tragedy* (Shakespeare's Globe – Sam Wanamaker Festival); *The Virtuous Burglar* (Buxton Fringe Festival). Television includes: *South Riding* (BBC). Radio includes: *And is There Honey Still For Tea?, Keep The Home Fires Burning* (Radio 4). Other work includes numerous audiobooks for Harper Collins.

Sophia Di Martino (*Emily Brontë*)
Theatre includes: *Finding Cole* (InTransit Tour); *Perhaps* (Greenroom); *Mania* (Michael Mayhew Co); *Dirty* (TransAction Theatre Co/Contact); *The Laramie Project* (Hope Theatre Co/Robert Powell Theatre); *4:48 Psychosis, Below the Text, deconstruction* (Salford University Studio); *A View from the Bridge* (Lakeview Centre). Television includes: *Eternal Law, Boy Meets Girl, The Royal Today, Strictly Confidential* (ITV); *The Road to Coronation Street* (BBC4); *Casualty, Doctors, Holby City, Survivors, New Street Law* (BBC1); *Spooks: Code 9, Ideal* (BBC3); *Heartbeat, The Marchioness Disaster* (YTV). Film includes: *Black Pond* (Black Pond Films); *Division* (Crazy Horse Films); *Blue, Free Range* (UK Film Council). This is Sophia's first production with Northern Broadsides.

Becky Hindley (*Lydia Robinson*)
Theatre includes: *Lisa's Sex Strike, Hamlet* (Northern Broadsides); *Martha, Josie and the Chinese Elvis* (Oldham Coliseum); *House of Bernarda Alba* (Nuffield Theatre); *Flamingoland, Kitty and Kate* (New Vic); *Double Death* (Mill At Sonning); *Jack Lear, Improbable Fiction, Playing God, My Sister Sadie, The Jollies, Mr A's Amazing Maze Plays* (Stephen Joseph); *Much Ado About Nothing* (Salisbury Playhouse); *Deathtrap* (No.1 tour for PW Productions); *House and Garden* (Northampton Royal Theatre); *Silly Cow* (Octagon Theatre Bolton); *Comic Potential* (Lyric, West End); *Captain of the Birds* (Abacus Theatre Company); *No Name* (Eastern Angles). Television includes: *Coronation Street, The Bill, Casualty, Doctors, Holby City, In Deep, The Peter Principle* and *People Like Us*. Radio includes: member of the Radio Drama Company; *Walter Now, Stone, Brief Lives, The Duchess of Malfi, Our Kath, Remains of the Day, Life is a Dream* and *A Town Like Alice*.

Rebecca Hutchinson (*Anne Brontë*)
Rebecca studied at Cambridge University before training at Mountview Academy of Theatre Arts. Theatre includes: *The Rise and Fall of Little Voice* (Dukes, Lancaster); *Jump* (Pleasance Dome, Edinburgh Festival); *Once Upon A Time at the Adelphi* (Union); *Beauty and the Beast* (Theatre Royal, Wakefield); *Closer than Ever* (Chelsea Theatre); The Wife/The Actress in the European Premiere of *See What I Wanna See* (ADC, Cambridge). Television includes: *Doctors* (BBC Television). Workshops include: *Festival 10 Masterclass* (Theatre Royal Haymarket, Janie Dee & Clive Rowe); *New and Contemporary Plays* (APS at the Royal Court, Jeremy Herrin); *High Comedy* (LAMDA, Maria Aitken); Fiona in *Slow Motion Suicide* (Leicester Square) Polly Van Dorsen in *Fairystories* (Grand Salon, Theatre Royal Drury Lane). This is Rebecca's first production for Northern Broadsides.

Catherine Kinsella (*Charlotte Brontë*)
Theatre includes: *The Tempest* (tour of China); *School For Scandal, The Bells, Macbeth, The Game* (Northern Broadsides); *Stepping Out, The Memory Of Water, On the Piste, Martha, Josie And The Chinese Elvis* (Coliseum, Oldham); *Noises Off* (Haymarket, Basingstoke/Coliseum, Oldham); *Turning Points* (M6 Theatre Company); *Low Pay? Don't Pay!* (Salisbury Playhouse); *The Maid Of Buttermere* (Theatre By The Lake, Keswick); *The Merchant Of Venice, The Crucible, Cleo, Camping, Emanuelle & Dick, A View From the Bridge* (Octagon Theatre Bolton); *Home Fires* (Dukes, Lancaster); *Double Act* (Watershed Productions/Polka); *The Night Before Christmas* (Big Wooden Horse Theatre Company). Catherine's professional debut was playing the role of Young Eponine in *Les Misérables* at the Palace Theatre, Manchester. Television includes: *Casualty, Waterloo Road, Boy Meets Girl, The Royal, Holby City* and *Doctors*. Radio includes: *The Janitor, The First Day of the Rest of My Life* (BBC Radio); *Chequebook and Pen* (Woolyback Productions); *In a Bamboo Grove, The Spring Sonata* (Watershed Productions).

Eileen O'Brien (*Tabby*)
Theatre includes: *Richard III* (MEN Award nomimation; Nothern Broadsides); *Macbeth*; '*Tis Pity She's a Whore, Rag and Bone* (Liverpool Best Actress Award), *Slung Low* (Liverpool Everyman); *When We Are Married* (TMA Award nomimation; West Yorkshire Playhouse/Liverpool Playhouse); *Death of a Salesman* (York Theatre Royal); *The Revenger's Tragedy, Basil and Beattie, Rafts and Dreams, Yerma, Across Oka* (TMA Award nomimation), *Prize Night, The Plough and the Stars* (Manchester Royal Exchange); *On the Shore of the Wide World* (Manchester Royal Exchange/National Theatre); *An Inspector Calls* (Coliseum, Oldham); *The Crucible, The Beauty Queen of Leenane* (MEN Award; Octagon Theatre Bolton); *A Doll's House; Kindertransport* (Liverpool Best Actress Award; Shared Experience); *Enjoy, Foxes* (West Yorkshire Playhouse); *Beyond Belief, Death of a Salesman* (Library, Manchester); *The Knocky, Redundant* (Royal Court, London). Television includes: series regular in *The Crezz, The Practice, The Nation's Health, How We Used to Live, No Bananas, And the Beat Goes On, Mersey Beat*. Leading roles in *The Sheikh of Pickersgill, One in a Thousand, The Last Company Car, Boys from the Blackstuff, The Vice, The Life and Crimes of William Palmer, The Life and Times of Henry Pratt, Rockliffe's Babies, Watching, Red in Tooth and Claw, Eyes Down, Building the Titanic, EastEnders, Coronation Street, Emmerdale, Brookside, Heartbeat, A Touch of Frost, The Bill, The Adventures of Sherlock Holmes, Doctors, The Royal, The Royal Today, Casualty, Holby City, Moving On, Lennon Naked*. Film includes: *A Private Function* (dir. Malcolm Mowbray); *A Month in the Country* (dir. Pat O'Connor); *Fanny and Elvis* (dir. Kay Mellor); *Runners* (dir. Charles Sturridge). Radio includes: numerous plays and short stories including a trilogy by Shelagh Delaney, *ID, Caligari, Legacy, Tin Man, Snow in July*.

Marc Parry (*Curate*)
Theatre includes: *Peter Pan* (Visible Fictions/National tour); *The Revenger's Tragedy, The Tempest, The Taming of the Shrew* (Manchester Royal Exchange); *Cinderella, Aladdin* (Pendle Productions/Thwaites Empire Theatre Blackburn); *Bare* (Ithaka Theatre Co/Coliseum, Oldham/tour). Television includes: *Bedlam, Emmerdale, Coronation Street, Hollyoaks, Spooks: Code 9*, and *Brookside*. Radio includes: *The Golden Notebook, Daisy* (Radio 4); *Bats in the Belfry* (BBC Radio Lancashire); *Five Lives* (Storm FM). This is Marc's first production with Northern Broadsides.

Barrie Rutter (*Teacher* & Director)
Rutter is the Founder and Artistic Director of Northern Broadsides. He was born in Hull and since leaving school in 1964 his acting career has stretched from Hamburg to Helsinki, Bradford to Beijing and includes film, television and radio. But he is best described as a 'theatre animal', and has had his happiest moments on the stage, whether in Shakespeare's Globe, London, or the ancient amphitheatre of Epidaurus. His theatre work includes: *Henry IV, Henry V, Coriolanus* and *The Taming of the Shrew* for the Royal Shakespeare Company and *The Mysteries, The Crucible, Guys and Dolls, The Oresteia, The Rivals, Animal Farm, Martine* and *The Trackers of Oxyrhynchus* for the Royal National Theatre. In 2008 Rutter directed and played the title role in the premiere of *Jack Lear* by Ben Benison at the Stephen Joseph Theatre, Scarborough, and directed *The Tempest* for THOC Cyprus Theatre Organisation. In 2009 he directed *Richard III* in Estonia for Theatre Vanemuine, Tartu, Estonia. Work for Northern Broadsides as director and actor includes: *Richard III, The Merry Wives, Poetry or Bust, A Midsummer Night's Dream, The Cracked Pot, The Blood of Dracula, The Passion, Romeo and Juliet, Antony and Cleopatra, Samson Agonistes, The Trackers of Oxyrhynchus, Twelfth Night, King Lear, The Mysteries 2000, Much Ado About Nothing, Alcestis, King John, Oedipus, Macbeth, Henry V, Antigone, The Merchant of Venice, Comedy of Errors, Sweet William, School for Scandal, The Wars of the Roses, The Man With Two Gaffers, The Tempest, Lisa's Sex Strike, Othello, Medea* and *The Game*.

Blake Morrison (Writer)
Blake Morrison was born in Skipton, Yorkshire, and educated at Nottingham University, McMaster University and University College, London. After working for the *Times Literary Supplement*, he went on to become literary editor of both the *Observer* and the *Independent on Sunday* before becoming a full-time writer in 1995. Since then, he has translated and adapted five hugely successful plays which were all commissioned and performed by Northern Broadsides Theatre Company: *The Cracked Pot* in 1996 (an adaptation of Heinrich von Kleist's *Der Zerbrochene Krug*); Sophocles' *Oedipus* in 2001; *Antigone* in 2003; *The Man with Two Gaffers*, a version of Carlo Goldoni's comedy *The Servant of Two Masters*, in 2006; and in 2007 *Lisa's Sex Strike*, which transforms Aristophanes' classic farce *Lysistrata*, into a contemporary comedy set in a northern mill town. Currently Professor of Creative Writing at Goldsmiths College, London, Blake is also a poet, novelist and journalist, who first came to public attention with his controversial collection *The Ballad of the Yorkshire Ripper*, but is more widely known for two family memoirs, *And When Did You Last See Your Father?* (which became a film starring Colin Firth, Juliet Stevenson and Jim Broadbent), and *Things My Mother Never Told Me*. His most recent book is a novel (his third to date), *The Last Weekend*, a psychological thriller set in East Anglia which came out in paperback earlier this year.

Conrad Nelson (Composer and Resident Director)
Conrad's acting career spans over twenty years and boasts a vast body of work in repertory and touring theatre and in radio, television and film. He has also built a reputation as a dramatic composer and has written music for theatre, television and radio. His longest association by far has been with Northern Broadsides as actor, Musical Director/composer on almost every Broadsides production and as Assistant Director on several major productions. For Northern Broadsides, work includes: *Othello, The Tempest, Wars of the Roses Trilogy, Sweet William, Comedy of Errors, Antigone, King John, The Merry Wives, Much Ado About Nothing, The Mysteries 2000, King Lear, The Trackers of Oxyrhynchus, Samson Agonistes, Romeo and Juliet, Antony and Cleopatra, A Midsummer Night's Dream, The Kaisers of Carnuntum* and *Poetry or Bust*; title roles in *Oedipus, Henry V* and *Richard III*. Other theatre includes work at The Royal National Theatre, The New Vic, Octagon Theatre Bolton, Lyric Hammersmith, Young Vic, and touring with companies such as Cheek by Jowl and Renaissance. Television includes: *The Street, Apparitions, Coronation Street, Without Motive* and *Only Fools and Horses*.

Radio includes: *The Mayor of Casterbridge, The Age of Innocence, The Paston Letters, Leona Cash, Richard III, Antony and Cleopatra, Hamlet* and *Ironhand*.

Films include: *Dancin' Thru the Dark, Much Ado About Nothing* and *The Stranger*. Conrad's directorial debut as Associate Director for Broadsides was Deborah McAndrew's acclaimed new adaptation of the famous gothic melodrama *The Bells* (2004), followed by *Vacuum* by Deborah McAndrew (2006), Blake Morrison's *Lisa's Sex Strike* (2007), *Accidental Death of an Anarchist* (2008), adapted by Deborah McAndrew, *The Canterbury Tales* (2010), adapted by Mike Poulton; George Orwell's *1984*, adapted by Nick Lane and *Hamlet* (2011). Other directing work includes *Oleanna* (2006) for The New Vic Theatre, Newcastle under Lyme, *A Christmas Carol* (2007) for the Octagon Theatre Bolton and *Vacuum* (2008) for Esk Valley Theatre.

Tim Skelly (Lighting Designer)
Tim Skelly is a resident theatre designer and academic at the Gulbenkian Centre, University of Hull. He has also worked as an academic at the Workshop Theatre, University of Leeds and as a resident practitioner and teacher of lighting design at the Royal Academy of Dramatic Art in London. As a freelance lighting designer professional work includes: *The Game* and *Wars of the Roses* for Northern Broadsides; *NHS* and *Union Street* for Plymouth Theatre Royal; *Time Gentlemen Please!* for The Demon Barbers; *Aladdin, Cinderella* and *Runaway Diamonds* for West Yorkshire Playhouse; *Ugly* and *Sex & Docks & Rock 'n' Roll, Bittersweet Sunshine* for Red Ladder Theatre Company; *Beached* and *Sit Bach and Enjoy* for Opera North; *Three Sisters* and *Romeo and Juliet* for Colchester Mercury Theatre; *Chiaroscuro, LUXURIA* and *High Land* for Scottish Dance Theatre; and technical management and lighting support for *Cattlecall, Picadores* and *Paseillo* for Phoenix Dance Theatre. Tim has also worked as a lighting consultant for Yorkshire Sculpture Park and has collaborated with several artists, including lighting designs for Sir Anthony Caro's *The Trojan Wars*, and retrospectives for Philip King and Christo.

Kraig Winterbottom (Sound Designer)
Kraig's design work includes: assistant video designer for Northern Broadsides' *1984*, assistant lighting design for Northern Broadsides' *Hamlet* and the video design for Derby University's *The Country Child*. Off the stage, Kraig shoots and directs cinematic trailers for theatre productions. His recent projects include the trailer for *Hamlet* for Northern Broadsides, *The BFG* for Derby LIVE, and also the trailer for *We are Three Sisters*.

Jessica Worrall (Designer)
For Northern Broadsides work includes: *Lisa's Sex Strike, Wars of the Roses, School for Scandal, The Bells, Macbeth, Twelfth Night, Oedipus, The Cracked Pot, King John, Antony and Cleopatra, A Midsummer Night's Dream, Richard III* and *The Merry Wives*. Also as a member of the performance group, The People Show, has designed, devised and occasionally performed in around nineteen shows including *The Ghost Sonata no. 119* (Sefton Park Glass House, Liverpool); *The Birthday Show no. 120; The Obituary Show no. 114* and *Baby Jane no.113* (all national tours). Other work includes: *Alice Through the Looking Glass* (Egg Theatre, Bath); *Huxley's Lab* (Grid Iron, Edinburgh); *Chekhov Shorts, Dangerously Yours* and *Arlechinno's Revenge* (all for Lung Ha's, Edinburgh); *Snow Queen* (Macrobert Stirling); *Turandot* (Festival Theatre, Edinburgh); *Peter Pan* (Theatre Royal, Bath). Film design includes: *Death of a Double Act* (directed by Christine Entwistle) and *A Loss of Sexual Innocence* (directed by Mike Figgis).

Photo © Nobby Clark

Standing (left to right)
**Jessica Worrall, Marc Parry, Eileen O'Brien, Barrie Rutter, Blake Morrison,
Becky Hindley, Bryony Rutter, John Branwell**
Seated (left to right)
**Gareth Cassidy, Catherine Kinsella, Rebecca Hutchinson, Sophia Di Martino,
Duggie Brown**

Northern Broadsides
Dean Clough
Halifax
HX3 5AX
Tel: 00 44 (0) 1422 369 704
www.northern-broadsides.co.uk

Board of Directors
Chair – Rachel L Harris
Anthony Gartland
Roger Harvey OBE
Frances Tighe BA (Hons) and LLB (Hons)

Supported by
**ARTS COUNCIL
ENGLAND**

Registered charity number 1076764

Friends of Northern Broadsides

We would like to thank the following for their generous support:

Mr T Ablett
Ms D Adlard
Mrs EA Ambler
J C Adamson
Ms M Anderson
Mr W W Anderson
Mr M Andrew
Mr & Mrs Archer
Miss M Arnall
Ms ML Arthur
Mr P Arthur
Mrs E Ashcroft
Mr D Ashton
Mr P Atkin
Mr H Atkin
Mr S Attridge
Mr RC Auty
Mrs P Bailey
Ms S Bailey
Dr J Bamford
Mrs B Barrett
Mr W Baugh
Mrs G Baxter
Mr R Baxter
Ms K Beevers
Mr F Benson
Mr M Bentley
Mrs E Beresford
Miss D S Berry
Mrs P Bickerton
Mr J Bishop
Mrs JA Bishop
Mr M Blackburn
Ms H Blundell
Mr C Booth
Mrs G Booth
Miss C Bowles
Mr C R Bratton
Mrs E A Bratton
Mrs J Bray
Mr J Brettell
Mrs P Brewster
Ms A Brickman
Mr Keith Briggs
Mr G Broadhead
Ms A Broadhead
Mrs G Brown
Ms H Brown
Mrs J Brown
Pat Brown
Mr P Brunyee
Miss M Burke
Mrs V Butcher
Dr C Butler
Mrs CE Calvert
S Chatterton
Mr D Child
Ms B Chorley
Mr M Clark
Mr J Coates
I Collinson
Mr J Comyn-Platt
Mr J Cone
Ms J Copley

Ms A Cornwell
Ms JM Cottrill
Mrs G Crawley
J Crick
Mr I Crosby
Ms E Crossley
Mr D Crowther
Mr R Crowther
Mrs JD Cullen
Mrs J Cunnington
Miss P Cunningham
Mrs L Curry
Mrs S Dale
Mrs E Darlington
Mr A Darnborough
Miss E Davnall
Mr R Delargy
Mr M S Demwell
Dr & Mr Duerden
Mr K Eames
Mrs A Edwards
Mrs H E Edwards
Mr S Evans
Ms R Eversley
Miss L Fairbairn
Mr & Mrs I Falconer
Mrs M Field
Ms S Fielden
Mrs J Finch
Ms R Flisher
Mrs E Foster
Ms J Fox
Mr A Foxton
Mr J Frearson
Mrs R Garside
Mr T Gartland
Mrs M Gibbons
Mrs M B Golightly
Mr R Golightly
Mr A Good
Mr D Goodfellow
Ms D Goodfellow
Mr C Gordon-Clark
H. Gothard
Mr P Goulden
Mrs C Grayshan
Ms H Green
Jean Greening-Jackson
Judy Green
Mr W Haggas
Mrs C Hall
Ms C Halsall
Katie Hale
Mr T Hardman
Mrs P Hargreaves
Mrs J Harris
Mr EP Harrison
Mr & Mrs DH Harrison
Mr P Harrison
Mrs L Harvey
Mr R Harvey
Prof G W Hastings

Mrs Nicky Healy
Mr D Henman
Dr Richard Herbert
Mrs N Heydon
Mr D Hill
Mr G Hill
Mrs L Hodge
Mr J Hoggard
Ms A Holling
Mr P Holling
Mr K Holroyd
Dr M Holtom
Mr P Hooker
Mr C Housley
Mr D Howl
Mr GH Hubbard
Mrs P Hubbard
Mr GL Hughes
Mr WJ Humphreys
Mrs E Hunt
Mr W Hurst
Ms C Hustwick
Mrs C Hutt
Mrs J Jack
Mrs P Jackson
Mrs S James
Mr B Johnston
Mr D Johnson
Mr David Johnson
Mrs JM Johnson
Dr JK Jones
Mrs J Jones
Mrs J Jowitt
Mr J Kearney
Mrs N Kellett
Mr D Kent
Mrs E Key
Mr SW Kilburn
Mrs H King
Anne Kirker
Tim Kirker
Ms C Langley-Wood
Mr J Leaf
Dr PM Lee
Mrs T Lee
Ms A Lister
Mrs I Lloyd
Mrs G Loftus
Mrs A Lomax
Ms S Luke
Mr T Mackrill
Mrs A Mahon
Miss G Mann
Mr John Martin
Ms SJ Maude
Mr J McAndrew
Mrs C McDonald
Mr N McDonald
Mrs E McMyn
Ms J Milner
Mr D Milnes
Mrs M Mitchell
Mr John Moran

Mr A Morris
Mr M Muller
Mrs W Munday
Ms CM Murphy
Mr D Narey
Mrs N Narey
Miss K Nethercoat
Mrs R Newman
Mrs L Newton
Mrs K Noble
Mrs J Normington
Dr J Norris
Mrs P Norris
Mr G O'Callaghan
Mrs A Oliver
Mr R Ormson
Prof I Oswald
Mr A Palethorpe
Mr D Palethorpe
Mrs M Palethorpe
Mr DJ Parker
Mr J C Peach
Mr C Pearce
Mr A Pennington
Mr J Pickles
Mrs S Pinder
Mr A Plater
Mrs S Platt
Mr MW Powell
Mrs J E Quinn
Ms P Read
Miss NM Richardson
Miss EJ Ridley
Mr GR Robson
Mr M Rogerson
Mr D Roper
Mrs MB Rotheray
Dr.P Ruffle
Mrs S Saunders
Mrs C Savage
Ms M Saxon
Ms L Saxton
Ms H Scoffin
Mr J Scott
Mr S R Scott
Dr J Senior
Mr P Sharp
Mrs P Sharp
Ms J Sharples
Ms M Sharples
Mr S Shaw-Wright
Ms Maddy Sheals
Mrs G Shepppard
Mr J Shoop
Mr J Sibbald
Mr J Siddle
Mr & Mrs Silburn
Mrs M Sinton
Ms AM Slade
Ms S Sloan
Mrs C A Smith
Dr PRS Smith
Mrs S Smith

Mrs L Spencer
Mrs A Spiers
Ms SJ Stephenson
Mrs H Stevens
Ms D Stirling-Chow
Ms V Stone
Mrs J Strapps
In memory of Mrs EM Spencer
Mr A Stratford
Ms C Sullivan
Ms R Sutchliffe
Mrs CM Teal
Miss KB Thompkins
Mrs S Thompson
Mrs F Tighe
Mr C Tombs
Mr C Toole
Mrs G Tordoff
Mrs M Turner
Miss Deborah Tynan
Mrs S M Verity
Ms C Walker
Mr & Mrs ST Walker
Mr & Mrs P Walker
Mrs G Walmsley
Mr S Walton
Mr N Ward
Mr KR Wark
Mrs S Watson
Mr & Mrs SR Watson
Miss S Watson
Ms L Wattis
Mrs N M Webb
Mr A Webster
Ms L Westbrook
Dr R Wheeler
Mr J Wheelwright
Mrs A Witcher
Mrs JS Whiteley
Mrs Kate Wilcock
Mr J Wild
Mr P Wilkinson
Miss AC Williams
Mrs J Willis
Ms H Wilson
Mrs K Wilson
Mr A J Wilson
Ms A Wood
Mr AK Wood
Miss M Woolfenden
Ms CJ Wright
Mr G Wright
Mrs R Yaldren
Mr AD Young
Mrs G Young
Mr M Young
Dr V Young

and all those Friends who wish to remain anonymous

To become a Friend of Northern Broadsides please visit
www.northern-broadsides.co.uk

WE ARE THREE SISTERS

Blake Morrison

Author's Note

Though much of the play is based on real events in the Brontës' lives, and some of the words spoken are ones they used, many alterations have been made, not least to chronology. The scheme for setting up a school, the bog-burst, the trip to London, Branwell's dismissal from his post as a tutor – all these things happened, but over a period of some years and not necessarily in the order shown here.

The curate is loosely modelled on William Weightman, but he was dead by the time the play is set. Lydia Robinson was a real person, with whom Branwell almost certainly had an affair, but she never visited him in Haworth. And though I have used the actual names of a teacher and doctor who were well-known to the Brontës – Ebenezer Rand and John Wheelhouse – their characters and behaviour are wholly invented.

We are Three Sisters uses the template of Chekhov's *Three Sisters* but in places departs radically from it – nothing resembling Act Four exists in the original.

Blake Morrison

Characters

PATRICK BRONTË
CHARLOTTE
EMILY
ANNE
BRANWELL
DOCTOR
CURATE
TEACHER
LYDIA ROBINSON
TABBY (*housekeeper*)

This text went to press before the end of rehearsals and so may differ slightly from the play as performed.

ACT ONE

Semi-darkness, candlelight, gravestones visible in the background – from which ANNE, CHARLOTTE *and* EMILY *emerge. They walk round and round a dining table, talking animatedly it seems. Slowly they take their places at the table.*

Lights come up. Morning. All three have a small writing desk in front of them.

CHARLOTTE. Mother died on a day like this. It was September, not your birthday, Anne. But a wind was blowing from the tops. You were a baby, Emily was three and I was five. I remember wondering what would become of us – if you'd ever survive. Now look at you. I remember them carrying the coffin out and the organ swirling from church and a handful of mourners, black as crows.

ANNE. I don't remember. I was too little to take it in.

CHARLOTTE. We'd barely arrived when she fell ill. We came in a dog cart with two wagons full of furniture trailing behind. There were daffodils in the garden and white clouds over the moor. We were all excited. We'd no idea what was coming.

ANNE. My first memory is gravestones. What's yours, Emily?

EMILY *whistles.*

CHARLOTTE. What are you reading?

ANNE. My diary paper. From four years back. I'd started working for Mrs Robinson. It makes me laugh to see how innocent I was.

CHARLOTTE. You must write your entry for today.

ANNE. I'm going to. I'll write about you and Emily and Father and Branwell, and all that's happened, even the bad things.

EMILY *whistles.*

CHARLOTTE. Do you have to whistle, Emily? I've a headache.

ANNE. You need a holiday. I'll come with you. We could go to London.

CHARLOTTE. To the opera house.

ANNE. And the National Gallery.

CHARLOTTE. And to see about getting our books published.

ANNE. Emily too. All three of us. And Branwell. He can show us the sights.

EMILY *whistles*.

I felt so happy waking up today, knowing it was my birthday. It was as if our mother was alive again. And Elizabeth and Maria. It was wonderful.

CHARLOTTE. You look lovely. So do you, Emily, if you weren't so gaunt. Branwell could be handsome, too, if he took more care of himself. I'm the one letting the family down. Look at me: not yet thirty and already an old maid.

ANNE. You could have married. You've been asked.

CHARLOTTE. Twice. But I hated the thought of sitting at home all day, with a grave face and a husband I'd no feelings for. And could you imagine me as a bride, all in white on a cold spring morning, like a snowdrop? What if I'd said yes, though? At least my health would be better. I'd not have to teach for a living.

Sound of gunshot.

Or hear Father fire his pistol every morning.

ANNE. Leave him be – he likes to keep his eye in.

CHARLOTTE. It's too late for that. His eyes are nearly gone.

Enter PATRICK.

Must you, Father? One of these days you'll hit someone.

PATRICK. There are starlings on the church tower.

CHARLOTTE. You're wrecking the masonry. And scaring the neighbours.

PATRICK. No one's complained.

CHARLOTTE. I'm complaining.

ANNE. You missed your vocation. You should have been a Cossack in the Russian army.

PATRICK. Emily doesn't mind, do you, my dear? I've been teaching her. She's a good eye.

EMILY *whistles*.

I've a wedding later.

CHARLOTTE. I thought you looked grumpy.

PATRICK. Most marriages are a crime against reason. And I hate being an accessory to crime.

ANNE. When people are in love, why shouldn't they marry?

PATRICK. Two poor beggars pooling their weaknesses, under the pretence of some fantastic tie of feeling, then quickly tiring of each other – that's marriage.

ANNE. Did you tire of Mother?

PATRICK. There wasn't time. We'd six young children to look after. Anyway, I forgot to tell you. The new curate is calling on us.

ANNE. A visitor – good.

CHARLOTTE. Not another curate! Remember the last one? He kept complaining that people from Yorkshire are uncouth. As if to impress us. Overlooking the fact we're from Yorkshire ourselves. Curates! They're the worst specimen of the male sex you'll ever meet. I don't care if I never see another curate for the rest of my life.

ANNE. What's he like, Father?

PATRICK. Well-mannered. Good sense of humour. His only fault is he talks too much.

ANNE. How old is he?

PATRICK. Thirty or so.

CHARLOTTE. Married?

PATRICK. Oh, he'll never marry.

CHARLOTTE *and* ANNE. Ah…

PATRICK. Women fall for him. And he's always falling in love himself…

CHARLOTTE. A lovesick curate. Heaven help us.

PATRICK. …but he's too tied to his sister to wed. From what I gather – and he's always telling folks about it – she's half out of her wits. Spends her life threatening to kill herself, just to annoy him. I don't know how he tolerates it.

Knock on door.

That'll be him now.

Enter DOCTOR.

DOCTOR. Morning, everyone.

ANNE. Oh, it's you.

DOCTOR. Now where did I put it? Mm…

Rummages in bag, withdraws bottle from it, and swigs.

New brand of tonic. Guaranteed to ward off consumption. Would you like a swig?

CHARLOTTE. Certainly not.

ANNE. Nor me. I've not had a cough in weeks. I'm so happy today. It's as if I were at sea in a fishing boat, with white gulls following, and blue sky all around.

DOCTOR. My little seagull.

ANNE. And you know why I felt happy? Because I realised what my purpose in life is: to work. It's why I envy weavers and millhands, farmers and railwaymen, because they've work to do. Real work. Just because we're women doesn't mean we can't work. You know that idea we once had? Let's do it. We must start a school.

CHARLOTTE. Oh, Anne. You know how you hated being a governess. We both did. The children are spoilt, the servants resent you, the parents think you unfit to share a table with them. It's drudgery, it's slavery, it's human bondage.

ANNE. Running a school will be different – we'll be in charge.

CHARLOTTE. There'll still be children. And you're no fonder of children than I am.

ANNE. I don't mind good ones.

CHARLOTTE. There's no such thing: they're either dunces or riotous cubs.

ANNE. We'll take day pupils – just eight to ten of them to start with. There'll be history lessons, writing, arithmetic, history, geography, needlework – and music and drawing for an extra guinea. We'll have cards made and send them out as far as... Dewsbury.

CHARLOTTE. You really have been dreaming.

ANNE. It's funny, I used to imagine us as three sisters on a big country estate, lazing in bed all morning and taking hours to get dressed. Now I realise what a boring life that would be. I'd rather be a collier or a pit pony. If we don't start our own school in the next year, doctor, you must promise not to be my friend.

DOCTOR. A friend? Certainly not. It's a promise.

CHARLOTTE. You make me laugh, Anne. I'm up at six every day, while Emily helps Tabby with the breakfast. Whereas you stay in bed till nine, with a dreamy look on your face.

ANNE. You never take me seriously. You treat me like a little girl. But I'm not. I'm an adult. And I want to work.

PATRICK. Idleness is a sin, you're right, Anne. It's like these men at the Health Board. How many times have I written to them about the state of the water? Do they ever reply? Have they ever sent an inspector? Lazy good-for-nothings: I'd like to shoot the lot of them. Twenty years from now, *everyone* will be working.

DOCTOR. I'll not be working.

PATRICK. You're a doctor. You don't count.

DOCTOR. I'll be dead by then.

PATRICK (*cleaning his pistol*). If you're not I'll put a bullet through your head.

DOCTOR. What kind of gun oil is that?

PATRICK. I don't know. I get it from Ireland.

DOCTOR. I use castor oil for my gun – the same stuff I give to patients.

PATRICK. I'm surprised you have any patients.

DOCTOR. You don't need many as long as they're rich.

ANNE. *We're* not rich. Why do you come to us?

DOCTOR. I'm a lonely old man, whose only comfort is visiting you girls. Which reminds me… It must be in my other bag. Excuse me a moment.

Exit DOCTOR.

ANNE. He's up to one of his tricks.

CHARLOTTE. It's no trick – he's bought you a present.

ANNE. I wish he wouldn't.

CHARLOTTE. It's obvious. He's infatuated.

EMILY (*sings/recites*).
'I see around me tombstones grey
Stretching their shadows far away.
Beneath the turf my footsteps tread
Lie low and lone the silent dead.'

ANNE. You're sad today, Emily.

CHARLOTTE. She's always sad.

EMILY (*putting on coat*). I'm going for a walk.

ANNE. It's cold out.

EMILY. I feel marooned – marooned on a sea of stones.

CHARLOTTE. It's your sister's birthday. And the curate's coming.

EMILY. I'll be back. (*To* ANNE.) Happy birthday, little one. I don't remember Mother, either. But if she were here to see you, she'd be proud. We'll have a good natter when I'm back. Walking always bucks me up.

CHARLOTTE (*displeased*). You're so wilful, Emily. Do you have to?

ANNE (*tearful*). It's all right. I understand.

PATRICK. I wish I understood. You girls make no sense at all.

EMILY. What are you talking about, Father?

PATRICK. You scribble away in your diaries and you read fat books and you philosophise – anybody would think you were men. Never forget that you're women, girls. Ah, someone in the hall. Must be the curate.

Enter TABBY, *carrying a cake*.

You're not the curate, Tabby. Where've you hidden him?

Exit PATRICK.

CHARLOTTE. That looks delicious, Tabby.

TABBY. It's not me who made it. A lad fetched it up from Mr Rand, at t'school.

ANNE. Thank you. Tell the lad I'm grateful.

CHARLOTTE. Shall we cut it now? You must have some, Tabby.

TABBY. Nay, it's too early in t'day for *my* belly. Never eat owt sweet till after dinner, I were told. And never draw t'curtains when sun's shining or it'll put the fire out.

ANNE. We don't have curtains. Father won't allow it.

TABBY. Aye, good job too.

Exit TABBY.

CHARLOTTE. It's a lovely cake.

EMILY. Mr Rand only sent it to get in our good books – so that we'll go and work for him. You didn't invite him here, did you?

ANNE. Of course not.

EMILY. Good.

Enter DOCTOR, *carrying a decanter*.

ANNE. A whisky decanter!

CHARLOTTE. You know Father doesn't hold with spirits.

DOCTOR. I've told him – whisky's good for his dyspepsia.

CHARLOTTE. He might allow himself a tot now and then – he doesn't need a great decanter.

DOCTOR. Use it as a water jug, then. I couldn't let Anne's birthday pass without buying her something. Haven't I known you since you were a baby? I used to hold you in my arms when your mother was ailing.

ANNE. But it's too expensive – it's cut-glass.

DOCTOR (*upset*). If I can't buy you a present on your birthday... Just put it away somewhere...

Enter PATRICK *with* CURATE.

PATRICK. Now this here's Charlotte, my oldest.

CHARLOTTE. Hello.

PATRICK. And Anne's my youngest.

ANNE. Hello.

PATRICK. And this is Emily, the middle one.

EMILY. The lovesick curate, eh.

CURATE. Sorry?... (*Seeing* EMILY*'s coat*.) Are you off somewhere?

ANNE. Emily loves to walk. She's worn twenty pairs of shoes out tramping the moors.

CURATE. Good for one's health, eh.

CHARLOTTE. Father's told us all about you.

CURATE. And he's told *me* all about *you*. The Miss Brontës. The three sisters. But he didn't do you justice. (*Sees cake*.) What are you celebrating?

ANNE. My birthday.

CURATE. Your birthday! If only I'd known.

PATRICK. You must have some. You'll be hungry if you've come from London.

ANNE. London!

CHARLOTTE. Anne hopes to visit London one day.

CURATE. It's a splendid place. So much to see.

CHARLOTTE. Were you born in London?

CURATE. No, I'm from Westmorland. But I'm often down there.

ANNE. Where do you stay?

CURATE. In Southwark. I can walk from my lodgings to the
    Abbey, over Westminster Bridge – do you know it? I stand in
    the middle and watch the barges passing below me and stare
    into the green depths as if I could lose myself in them. What
    a wide, wonderful river the Thames is. But you've such fine
    rivers here, too. What a place to live!

CHARLOTTE. It's cold and dreary.

ANNE. The wind never stops blowing.

EMILY. And there are midges.

CHARLOTTE. Nothing ever happens – we're buried away
    from the world.

CURATE. But it's so invigorating... The moors, the tarns. And
    the heather, of course. Marvellous. Only it's strange the
    nearest railway station is Keighley. Why is that?

DOCTOR. It's obvious. If it were nearer it wouldn't be so far.

    Puzzled silence.

CURATE. No, indeed.

CHARLOTTE. The doctor is just passing.

DOCTOR. I've known you girls since you were tots, haven't I,
    Anne.

ANNE (*ignoring him*). Branwell's been to London.

CHARLOTTE. Or says he has.

ANNE. Branwell's our brother. He'd plans to train as a painter.

CHARLOTTE. Mother stopped off in London, on her way from
    Penzance.

ANNE. I'd forgotten that.

EMILY. I've forgotten Mother.

CURATE. It's everyone's fate, I'm afraid. We'll all be forgotten.

CHARLOTTE. Great writers and artists aren't forgotten.

CURATE. Not their works, perhaps. But the men themselves. And even if they *are* remembered, they never know it. Weren't the discoveries of Galileo, say, or Isaac Newton, ridiculed in their lifetime? Whereas the cranks and fools of the day were taken seriously.

DOCTOR. There's many a fool still listened to today.

CURATE. Precisely my point. Who can say which names will survive for posterity? Who is there among writers from the past? Only Shakespeare, Milton and Jane Austen.

CHARLOTTE. Jane Austen! Oh, I know the whole world esteems her. But there's no open country in her work.

ANNE. No fresh air.

EMILY. No running becks.

CHARLOTTE. It's all neat borders and dainty flowerbeds. It's so narrow.

CURATE. Name me a living writer who's as good.

CHARLOTTE. I'm sure there are some.

ANNE. Even if they're not yet published.

EMILY. Or they choose to stay anonymous.

CHARLOTTE. Writers whose work will last for ever.

CURATE. Who can judge? We've no perspective. Is this is a Great Age or a minor one? It's too early to say.

DOCTOR. It can't be a Great Age, when the likes of me get to be doctors.

A flute can be heard offstage.

ANNE. That's Branwell playing. Father would have liked him to be a parson. But he's too much of an artist.

CHARLOTTE. He behaves like an artist. You never know what mood he'll be in.

ANNE. He's been working in York, for the same family I used to work for.

CHARLOTTE. They've given him leave for a month.

ANNE. They never gave me leave. *And* they pay him twice as much.

CHARLOTTE. He's good with children – he's a child himself, that's why.

ANNE. Remember the games we used to play with him. (*To* CURATE.) This house was once full of soldiers, you know.

CURATE. Really?

ANNE. There were three sets, in wooden boxes. We made up stories about them. Father bought them for Branwell as birthday presents.

Enter BRANWELL.

BRANWELL. What's that?

PATRICK. This is William, Branwell. My new curate.

ANNE. He's just come from London.

BRANWELL. London! You'll get no peace from my sisters, then.

CURATE. I hear you know London.

BRANWELL. Like the back of my hand.

CURATE. A man can never tire of the place.

BRANWELL. *I* did. I used to think that to spend a week roaming the British Museum would be paradise. Now if I saw the Elgin Marbles my eyes would be dull as a dead codfish.

ANNE. Branwell painted this picture of us.

CURATE. Yes, it's… most handsome.

ANNE. He put himself in to start with then rubbed the image out. You can still his shadow, look.

BRANWELL. You're embarrassing me. (*Starts to slip away.*)

ANNE. He paints and he's musical and he writes poetry. But he's a shadow. He will keep disappearing. (*Drags him back.*)

BRANWELL. I'm tired. I couldn't sleep. I sat up reading Horace's *Odes*.

CURATE. You know Latin, then?

BRANWELL (*distracted*). And Greek. Father taught me. And Keighley Library has a good classics section. Anyway...

ANNE. What's wrong with you? You're hopping about like a robin in a wormery.

CHARLOTTE. Are you expecting someone?

BRANWELL. I'm fagged. I need to lie down.

Exit BRANWELL.

CURATE. A Latin scholar – impressive. I expect you three sisters are clever, too.

CHARLOTTE. 'Clever' – I hate the word, applied to our sex. Noisy, ugly and meddling, you mean.

CURATE. Not at all. You're all most... charming.

CHARLOTTE. Even worse! Be charming to a man, instead of acting coldly and looking like marble, and you'll be accused of trying to hook him into marriage.

CURATE (*embarrassed*). No, I didn't mean...

EMILY. Charlotte and I studied French in Brussels. But there's no call for foreign languages in Haworth. It's a useless talent – like having a sixth finger on your hand. (*Looks ready to exit.*)

CURATE. Forgive me for disagreeing. But there's no place on earth where being educated is useless. What's the population of Haworth – six thousand or so? Mostly mill workers and factory hands, am I right? A rough and illiterate people, in other words. But let's suppose that of those six thousand there are three like you spreading enlightenment. Of course you can't raise working people to your level overnight. And at times you'll be swallowed in the mass, as if your efforts counted for nothing. But you'll leave an impression. And after you've gone there won't be three like you but six, then twelve, and so on, until finally you and your kind aren't a tiny enclave but the majority. A hundred years from now, life here in Haworth will be unimaginably beautiful. Everyone will have jobs and homes, everyone will have culture, everyone will be busy reading books. We all long for that, and dreaming of it, working at it, preparing the ground for it is the purpose of our existence. So don't tell me that being educated is useless.

Pause.

EMILY (*taking off her coat*). I'm stopping for dinner.

ANNE. Someone ought to have written that down.

DOCTOR. He's only saying what you said earlier: we all have to work. Even me.

CHARLOTTE. You do work. You have to. There's so much disease.

DOCTOR. I'm not saying I'm totally idle. But my methods are the same as they always were.

CURATE. What a lovely home. I do envy you. Since I left university, all I've known is dingy lodgings. To have a house like this – how lucky you are.

DOCTOR. There's so much new research. It's hard to keep up.

CHARLOTTE. The house belongs to the church. If Father died, we'd have nothing.

ANNE. That's why we have to work. So we can fend for ourselves.

DOCTOR. I sometimes think I should retrain and do something else.

CURATE. Yes, I often wonder what it would be like to start over again. Suppose the life we've been living is just a rough draft and we could throw it away and write a new version, like a fair copy. People say they'd not change a thing, but I know I would. I'd change the setting for a start – I'd want a house like this, with a fire in the hearth and purple hills all round. My sister's not well and things are difficult... Next time I'll come back as an only child.

Enter TEACHER.

TEACHER (*to* ANNE). Happy birthday, my dear Miss Brontë. Let me congratulate you on this auspicious occasion, this annual rite of passage, this momentous milestone on the bridleway of life. You did get the cake I sent?

ANNE. Yes, thank you.

TEACHER. I'd like to give you this as well: a short history of the school I established, written by myself. I know my prose can't compete with those novels you're so fond of reading, but I trust the contents will be instructive nevertheless – and perhaps persuade you to come and work for me.

PATRICK. This is William, my new curate.

TEACHER (*to* CURATE). Ebenezer Rand, principal of the school here. (*To* ANNE.) You'll find the name of every child enrolled for the past two years. *Feci quod potui faciant meliora potentes*: I have done what I could; let others take up the reins and do better.

ANNE. You gave me this for my last birthday.

TEACHER. Really? Well, let the curate have it. Here, have this with my compliments. Shall I sign it for you? You'll find it fascinating.

CURATE. Thank you.

TEACHER. I've a hundred and seventy pupils, currently.

CURATE. Must keep you busy.

TEACHER. Very busy. But I get lonely too. It's not good for a man to be alone.

CURATE. Why not take a wife?

TEACHER. Oh, I have a wife. It's a mistress I'm after.

ANNE *and* CHARLOTTE. 'A mistress'!

TEACHER. To teach the girls, while I teach the boys. Now if one of your daughters would oblige me, Reverend Brontë...

PATRICK. That's for them to decide.

EMILY. And we've decided no.

Awkward pause. Enter TABBY, *who starts to lay the table.*

CURATE. Look at the time, I'd better leave you to your celebrations.

CHARLOTTE. You're not off already?

ANNE. Stay and eat with us.

CHARLOTTE. You must.

CURATE. It's a birthday party. I'm intruding.

ANNE. Not at all.

CURATE. If you insist.

TEACHER. Yes, if you insist... (*Sits down.*) *Mens sana in corpore sano*, eh: a man must eat, the Ancient Greeks knew that. I've organised a walk for the children later: the fresh air will do them good. You'll come, Charlotte, won't you? Anne and Emily, too. Nothing too strenuous. I've measured it out: two miles and three hundred and eighty-five yards. Sit down, curate.

ANNE. There'll be enough for everyone. Tabby's made meat pie.

DOCTOR. Meat pie, excellent.

TEACHER. You must visit my school, William. It's the envy of every headmaster in the West Riding. Are you not eating, Patrick?

PATRICK. Of course. It's Anne's birthday. Don't suck that pencil, Charlotte. You'll give yourself lead poisoning. No wonder you look so pale. What have you been writing?

CHARLOTTE. Just a letter.

PATRICK. Who to?

CHARLOTTE. No one important. I'll show it you later.

ANNE (*to* DOCTOR). You can eat with us, too, but no more swigging whisky.

DOCTOR. Whisky calms me down. That curate gets on my nerves.

ANNE. Don't be silly. Not another drop, do you hear.

DOCTOR. All right, all right. I barely touch the stuff these days.

EMILY. Did you hear Mr Rand going on? Trying to organise us all? A walk with him and a bunch of schoolchildren? It's a hateful idea. He must be mad.

DOCTOR (*to* ANNE). I thought Emily liked walking.

ANNE. She does. But on her own, not in a gaggle. Come on, let's eat.

DOCTOR. Stay a second. (*Pause.*) What are you thinking about?

ANNE. Nothing special.

DOCTOR. I wish I knew what you were thinking. I know I'm old, in your eyes, but where love's involved...

ANNE. Don't talk about love.

DOCTOR. I could make you happy, you know.

ANNE. Could any man do that?... It's hard for us three, you know. We feel like weeds in a kitchen garden. And when we step outside, it's not cobbles we walk on, it's graves. Slab on slab, look. See the ones standing upright? They're like new graves sprouting from the old. First there was Mother, then Maria, then Elizabeth. Who'll be next? (*Tearful.*) I'm sorry... I was crying with happiness earlier and now look. I'm the youngest and everyone babies me. They think I've no judgement. But it'll be different once we start our school. You know how when it's hot in summer, and you're out walking, and you long for a cold beck you can duck your face in and drink and drink – that's the way I long for work.

Sound of door slamming.

You go ahead.

DOCTOR *joins others at the table.*

Enter BRANWELL *and* LYDIA.

Mrs Robinson!

LYDIA. Hello, Anne.

ANNE. I never thought to see you here.

LYDIA. I was passing... on my way to Scarborough.

ANNE. Have you brought the children?

LYDIA. No. It's just me.

BRANWELL. Lydia's stopping at The Black Bull.

LYDIA. Just for a day or two.

ANNE. Oh. I see.

LYDIA. I'm looking forward to meeting all your family. Your sisters especially.

ANNE. I'm sure they'll be... honoured.

BRANWELL. You've been crying, Anne.

ANNE. Too much excitement. It's my birthday.

LYDIA. Of course it is. How silly of me to forget. Do you like my fur?

ANNE. Yes, it's... it's... it's not fox, is it?

LYDIA. Fox is so common. No, this is mink, my dear.

ANNE. Don't let Emily see it. She's passionate about animals.

Enter CHARLOTTE.

CHARLOTTE. Aren't you coming for dinner, Anne?

ANNE. Charlotte, this is Mrs Robinson.

LYDIA. Delighted.

ANNE. She's on her way to Scarborough.

CHARLOTTE. Scarborough? You'll not get there from here.

LYDIA. I thought I'd call on Anne. For old times' sake.

BRANWELL. I've booked a room for Lydia...

CHARLOTTE. Mrs Robinson, you mean.

BRANWELL. Aye. She's stopping at The Black Bull.

ANNE. I'll go and tell Father.

Exit ANNE.

CHARLOTTE. You're wearing bright green.

LYDIA. Is that unlucky?

CHARLOTTE. We're a little less... colourful in this house.

LYDIA. I bought it in York. Suits my complexion, don't you think. Is there a mirror somewhere?

CHARLOTTE. Dinner's meat pie. I'll ask Tabby to set an extra place.

Exit CHARLOTTE.

LYDIA (*fussing with hair in mirror*). She doesn't like me.

BRANWELL. She'll be fine once she knows you. It was the same last time.

LYDIA. What do you mean, last time?

BRANWELL. There was a girl I... Who had my... Doesn't matter.

LYDIA. It's as if she's sitting in judgement. Or green dresses were a crime.

BRANWELL. Don't get upset, my love. The real world's a mystery to my sisters. But they read poetry and make up stories and though they haven't my talent they're not far behind. They might look strange – Charlotte's a dwarf, Emily's skinny as a rake, and Anne, well, you know Anne, she's nothing, absolutely nothing. But there's no malice to them.

LYDIA. I thought Haworth would be like Harrogate. But it's so remote. And so uncivilised. Those dirty women by the well were staring at me when the coach drew up...

CHARLOTTE (*calling*). Branwell!

BRANWELL. Come here where they won't see us. We'll have a perfect week together. And when you're free and we're married, we'll be happy forever more. I've never loved anyone as I've loved you.

They kiss.

CHARLOTTE *and* ANNE *stand watching them.*

End of Act One.

ACT TWO

Evening. The room is dimly lit. BRANWELL *sits in a chair, reading. Enter* LYDIA.

LYDIA. Hello! Anyone home? *There* you are. Reading again. Is that all anyone does in this house? I thought you'd be down to see me.

BRANWELL. We spent all day together.

LYDIA. Even so.

BRANWELL. My sisters will get suspicious.

LYDIA. Why? You're my children's tutor.

BRANWELL. If your gardener goes blabbing to your husband then I won't be much longer.

LYDIA. Don't be silly.

BRANWELL. We were seen together in the boathouse. And now you're here.

LYDIA. Are you sorry I came?

BRANWELL. Of course not. But what will your husband think?

LYDIA. I know how to deal with Edward. It's me who should be worrying, not you.

BRANWELL. Why, my love?

LYDIA. About catching a chill. The inn is so grubby and the bed there so cold. I was thinking... Couldn't Anne and Charlotte share, then I'd have a bedroom here, close to yours? Just for a night or two. Will you ask them?

BRANWELL. They're not here. They're out inspecting premises for their school.

LYDIA. Poor dears. Women shouldn't have to work.

BRANWELL. My sisters like to pay their way.

LYDIA. They need some fun in their lives... I've asked some musicians to come.

BRANWELL. What?

LYDIA. A troupe of musicians are staying at the inn. I've asked them to come up and play for us. It's my little treat.

BRANWELL. When's this?

LYDIA. Tonight.

BRANWELL. Tonight!

LYDIA. I said to come at nine.

BRANWELL. My father'll be in bed by nine.

LYDIA. He won't object then.

BRANWELL. My sisters will. You should have asked them first.

LYDIA. They like music, I know they do. Anne used to play the piano for my children. She's so sweet. I'm sure if you asked her to share rooms with Charlotte...

Enter TABBY.

TABBY. Albert Ferrier's outside.

BRANWELL. What's he want at this hour?

TABBY (*handing him a note*). He were here earlier but you were out.

BRANWELL (*reading the note*). Did he talk to my father?

TABBY. Not that I know of.

BRANWELL. Or my sisters?

TABBY. No.

BRANWELL. Well, don't say a word. Tell Albert I'll be with him.

Exit TABBY.

LYDIA. What's the matter?

BRANWELL. It's a man claiming I owe him money.

LYDIA. The cheek! Send him away.

BRANWELL. Trouble is, I maybe do owe him.

LYDIA. 'Maybe'?

BRANWELL. I had a drink or two and a hand of cards the other night, and, well, I know I lost a bob or two, but there's an IOU here, in my hand, for a lot more.

LYDIA. One should always be prompt at settling with tradesmen. You'd better pay up.

BRANWELL. I can't. I've not the money about me.

LYDIA (*snatches note*). Here, give it me. Goodness, that *is* a lot. Tabby! Really, Branwell. Don't you know how to play cards?

BRANWELL. Albert kept topping my glass up.

LYDIA. I'll teach you how to use guile. Tabby! Tabby! Oh, she's *so* slow, that woman, you should have got rid of her years ago.

Enter TABBY.

Now, Tabby, what's this Mr Ferrier fellow like? (*Takes money from purse.*)

TABBY. A wrong 'un. He's from Bradford.

LYDIA. Have you ever been to Bradford, Tabby?

TABBY. Nay, and my toes will be turning up afore I do.

LYDIA (*handing money over*). Well, tell him he should have more honour than to fleece young men of their hard-earned savings.

Exit TABBY.

BRANWELL (*kissing* LYDIA *and laughing*). 'Have you ever been to Bradford, Tabby?' She's never even been to Keighley.

LYDIA. People here live such narrow lives.

BRANWELL. Not me. I like Bradford. And Liverpool. I like all cities. I walk around without knowing anyone or anyone knowing me, and yet I feel at home. Whereas in Haworth I know everyone but they treat me like a stranger. If you live among secluded hills you never learn who you are. That's why I want to go away with you.

LYDIA. If Edward divorced me I'd be ruined. I've told you – we must wait till he dies.

BRANWELL. It could take years.

LYDIA. Don't be silly. You know how poor his health is. That's why he's jealous of you – you're young and strong.

BRANWELL. What's the use of being young if I can't have you?

LYDIA. Shhh. Just be patient.

They kiss; then, hearing voices, stop.

Exit BRANWELL *and* LYDIA. *Enter* EMILY *and* CURATE.

EMILY. I'll tell Father you're here.

CURATE. Don't bother him. He'll be busy writing his sermon.

EMILY. You must be starved.

CURATE. No, I ate in town.

EMILY. Cold, I mean – we're all cut up by this cruel east wind.

CURATE. I'm fine. A cup of tea would do me.

EMILY. Tabby's got the kettle on.

CURATE. Excellent. I approve of Tabby. Servants like her must be hard to find.

EMILY. We don't think of her as a servant. She's been with us since I was six. She can be blunt but she's a gentle soul.

CURATE. Oh, I'm all for bluntness. The rich and educated seem to think it's vulgar to talk plainly. But strip away the fancy phrases and their story's just the same as everyone else's – they're tired and off colour, the weather's bad, their children are a handful, their wives are wearing them out with their demands...

EMILY. What about the husbands wearing out the wives with *their* demands?

CURATE. True enough. *Everyone's* worn out. Even I am. It's the duty of a curate to offer hope. But when I see the conditions people live in here. And the lack of sanitation. One privy to twenty-four houses – it's a disgrace.

EMILY. Father wants them to put in sewers and piped water. We're lucky, we've a well. But the water most people drink runs down from the moors through the graveyard, where corpses are rotting. No wonder there's disease. Father's been complaining about it for years.

CURATE. He's a good man. But only the Chartists can redeem the poor. People want a say in things. But until they've the right to vote, they don't have a voice. It's no wonder there've been riots...

EMILY. Father doesn't approve of violence.

CURATE. Nor do I. If I'm in the pulpit, I preach forbearance. Love your neighbour and say your prayers, I tell them, then in the next life God will reward you. But some people aren't willing to wait that long. They want their reward in this life. The right to vote, a decent wage, better sanitation, free medicine for the sick – is that too much to ask? Sorry for rambling. Truth is, my sister's not well. We've only just got here and already she wants to move. We were arguing about it just now and I walked out. Her mind's not right. I worry what she'll do to herself. Forgive me, I've never talked about this to anyone. You're the only person I dare be honest with. (*Clasps her hand.*) You're not angry with me, are you?

EMILY. Do you hear that noise?

CURATE. It's the wind.

EMILY. Not just the wind. Listen. There. It's the mason with his chisel, chipping out another headstone.

CURATE. At this hour? It can't be.

EMILY. They're the two sounds we grew up with. The chip-chip-chip of the mason. And the wind whistling off the tops.

CURATE. You make the place sound haunted.

EMILY. It is. It's like living inside a coffin. Even in daylight, the air's as black as soot. And when it rains, it's like Indian ink spilling down.

CURATE. It may be dark but I can see your eyes shining.

EMILY. Shall I light another candle?

CURATE. No need, your eyes are brightness enough. There's a kindling to them, a glow, as if they were burning coals...

EMILY (*laughs*). Dying embers, maybe.

CURATE. I dreamt about you, you know. Last night and the night before. Oh dear, someone's coming.

Enter ANNE *and* DOCTOR.

DOCTOR. I heard you'd been unwell.

ANNE. No, just tired. Charlotte and I walked to Halifax and back.

DOCTOR. You should have told me. I'd have taken you in my dog cart.

ANNE. We were looking for premises for our school. But when we got there the husband was out, and his wife was too suspicious to show us round.

DOCTOR. I'm not surprised. You don't look old enough to start a school.

EMILY. You've lost weight since you had that cough, Anne. You *do* look young.

CURATE. Yes, and pretty too.

DOCTOR. It's the way you have your hair.

ANNE. Sometimes I wonder if our scheme is worth the effort. What if running a school turns out to be as boring as everything else? I want to feel busy, alive, inspired. The only time I *am* inspired is at night, when Father's in bed, and Emily, Charlotte and I sit by the fire and read out each other's...

EMILY (*quickly*). Where's Tabby with that tea? Would you two remind her we're waiting.

Exit DOCTOR *and* CURATE.

Don't tell them about our writing.

ANNE. But we'll be published soon. And once our books are out...

EMILY. No one will know *we* wrote them. That's the whole idea. Currer, Ellis and Acton – remember.

ANNE. Can't we tell friends?

EMILY. Which friends? Who?

ANNE. Well, Father and Branwell anyway.

EMILY. You know we can't. How many times do I have to tell you? Not even Father and Branwell, right.

ANNE. Right.

EMILY. Promise?

ANNE. Promise.

EMILY. Good... Albert Ferrier was here, for Branwell. I don't know why.

ANNE. It's all over town. Branwell lost at cards. They say he owes fifty pounds.

EMILY. Fifty pounds! That's half what he earns in a year. You'd think with Mrs Robinson here, he'd behave himself.

ANNE. He's worse with her around.

EMILY. She doesn't seem to mind. Whatever he does, she still dotes on him.

ANNE. That's how it was at Thorp Green.

EMILY. I don't understand. What's a woman like Mrs Robinson want from a younger man?

Enter DOCTOR *and* CURATE.

DOCTOR. We couldn't find Tabby. And I'm parched.

CURATE. I'd give my life for a cup of tea and a currant bun.

ANNE. She'll be outside. I'll go and fetch her.

Exit ANNE.

CURATE. Well, if we can't have tea, let's have a contest, doctor.

DOCTOR. Good idea. How about arm-wrestling? I can lift three hundred pounds, you know.

CURATE. A debate, I meant. A battle of wits.

DOCTOR. Oh, that... Well, all right, then.

CURATE. Now, I think we agree ours is an age of progress.

DOCTOR. Do we?

CURATE. So try to imagine what life will be like long after we're dead – in two hundred years, say, in the twenty-first century.

DOCTOR. All right... In two hundred years, people will fly to and from work in balloons. Women will wear trousers and men will wear skirts. And the sixth sense will be discovered, and scientists will find ways to use it. But to all intents life will be the same – hard graft for everyone, even doctors, with mysteries we can't fathom and mishaps we can't prevent and islands of happiness amid oceans of suffering. And that won't change even in a thousand years.

CURATE. But life *does* change – it's changing before our eyes, with the railways and industry and the Chartists and the revolutions brewing in Europe. And that's just the start. It may take two hundred years or even a thousand, but one day life will be glorious. Of course, we won't be around to enjoy it but our efforts will make it possible.

DOCTOR. That's supposing we make an effort. Not everyone does.

EMILY (*laughing*). No.

CURATE. It's our purpose on earth: to make things better for our descendants – if not our children, then our children's children's children. Our own happiness doesn't count.

DOCTOR. But what if I am happy?

CURATE. You're not.

DOCTOR. How do you know?

EMILY *laughs*.

What's up with you, today? I could sneeze and you'd find it funny. (*To* CURATE.) You're wrong. Life can't change because nature never changes. Every autumn the swallows leave and fly south, then every spring they come back again.

No one knows why they do it or how they find their way.
And no one ever will know. But they fly off and fly back
again year on year and they always will.

EMILY. But there must be some meaning.

DOCTOR. Look outside: it's dark. Where's the meaning in that?

EMILY. How can we live and not want to know why swallows
migrate or children die of disease or stars shine at night? If
we don't know why we're here, there's no point being
here… everything's just bare earth and empty skies.

Pause.

CURATE. All the same, I'm sorry my youth's nearly gone.

DOCTOR. What's that got to do with it?

EMILY.
'I'll not weep, because the summer's glory
Must always end in gloom;
And follow out the happiest story
It closes with a tomb!'

CURATE. Whose poem is that?

EMILY. I can't remember.

DOCTOR. You're totally baffling, you two. (*Sits down.*) What's
in the newspaper?

CURATE. Whoever the author is, it's morbid. You shouldn't
read gloomy verse.

EMILY. Gloom bucks me up – there's nothing more cheering
than a tale of woe. It's like the moors. People say *they're*
gloomy. But I love it up there – the heather, the bilberries,
the linnets, the curlews, and bog cotton and butterwort and
cowslips pushing up through the grass.

(*Recites.*)
'There is a silent eloquence
In every wild bluebell,
That fills my softened heart with bliss
That words could never tell.'

DOCTOR. 'The Poet Laureate celebrated his birthday at home in Rydal Mount yesterday.' Very interesting. I've been thinking of changing professions, you know.

EMILY. What, you're going to be a poet?

DOCTOR. No. I want a job so physically tiring that when I get home I'll be out like a light. Work, work, work – that's what my little Anne says, don't you, pet.

Enter ANNE.

ANNE. I'm not little and I'm not your pet. Tea's on its way.

CURATE. How old are you, doctor?

DOCTOR. Me? Thirty-two.

CURATE. There's that noise again.

EMILY. It's just the wind. No stopping it. The wind blows where it wants to.

ANNE. I'm sick of hearing it. I've forgotten what summer's like.

EMILY. We're like grasshoppers in this house, singing all summer and starving all winter.

DOCTOR (*reads from paper*). 'A new outbreak of smallpox in Salford has claimed at least fifty lives.'

Enter TABBY.

TABBY. Tea's up. Do you take milk, Mr…? Sorry, I've forgotten your name.

ANNE. William. And he does.

CURATE. Buttered scones – splendid.

TABBY. Eh up, look what's dropped out of the rookery. He can smell my baking three miles off.

Enter LYDIA *and* BRANWELL; *awkward pause.*

ANNE. Mrs Robinson. You've not left for Scarborough then…

LYDIA. Has anyone ever noticed how intelligent babies are? Perhaps it's just mine, but I remember saying 'good morning' to my son when he was just a baby, and him looking up at me in such a special way that I knew he'd understood. Forgive me, I must sound like a doting mother, but he really is the most gifted child, isn't he, Branwell?

TABBY. Aye, well, t'children in *this* house are gifted, but there's no use in having gifts if you waste 'em.

Exit TABBY.

LYDIA. She really is rude, that woman.

BRANWELL. She doesn't mean it.

LYDIA. I don't know how you put up with her.

BRANWELL. She's been with us since we were little.

LYDIA. She needs a good talking-to. Are you afraid of her or something?

BRANWELL. Lydia, please…

LYDIA. If you won't tell her, then I will.

Exit LYDIA, *flouncing off; exit* BRANWELL, *in pursuit*.

EMILY. Hear that wind. They say it drives horses mad. I must be a horse.

ANNE. If we lived in London the weather wouldn't matter. We'd not even notice if it was summer or winter.

DOCTOR. It's not just the weather you'd stop noticing. After a bit, you'd stop noticing London.

CURATE. London's unforgettable – I'd love to show you. Such enthralling sights wherever one goes.

DOCTOR. Twaddle. Who scoffed the scones?

ANNE. Must have been Branwell.

DOCTOR. All of them?

Enter TABBY.

TABBY. Note for you, sir.

CURATE. For me? (*Reads.*) It's from my sister. Right… Excuse me. You can have my scone, doctor.

DOCTOR. I don't want your damn scone.

CURATE (*agitated; in private to* EMILY). Another episode, I'm afraid.

EMILY. What's happened?

CURATE. My sister. She's ill again. Or says she is. I'd better go.

EMILY. Take the doctor with you.

CURATE. She'll be making it up. She always does.

EMILY. She must be lonely. Bring her here – we've still not met her.

CURATE. I'll see.

Exit CURATE.

TABBY. He's not had his tea. What's up with him?

DOCTOR. He's got midges in his britches, that one.

TABBY. I'm stalled of curates.

DOCTOR. He talks as if every other man were beneath him.

EMILY (*angry*). Leave William alone! Stop interfering.

TABBY. I meant no harm, love.

EMILY. I know *you* didn't.

BRANWELL (*voice from offstage*). Tabby!

TABBY (*mimicking*). 'Tabby!' What's he want this time?

Exit TABBY.

ANNE. Are you all right?

EMILY. Don't touch me. I'm fine.

DOCTOR. It must be flu, Emily. You seem heated.

EMILY. The thing about you, doctor, is that you will talk tripe.

DOCTOR. Ooh, I fancy some tripe. Tripe and onions. With a large whisky to follow. Any whisky in the house?

Enter PATRICK.

PATRICK. Did someone mention tea?

DOCTOR. Patrick, old son. Where've you been? Cranking out your sermon? What's the theme? Sins of the flesh again?

PATRICK. That was last Sunday.

DOCTOR. Doesn't mean it won't be this Sunday. Here's a story for you. 'Colonel shot dead in a duel in Camden Town.'

PATRICK. It's a criminal waste.

EMILY. Lord Wellington once fought a duel.

PATRICK. No, he didn't go through with it. No one died.

DOCTOR. But when a man insults you... or tries to steal what's rightly yours...

PATRICK. ...then turn the other cheek. Duelling's an abomination. I've written to the *Leeds Mercury* about it.

ANNE. You have your pistol, Father.

PATRICK. For protection. These Chartist hotheads worry me. There've been riots in Bingley. I remember the last time, with the Luddites.

DOCTOR. How about a drop of Dutch courage?

PATRICK. You know I don't drink.

DOCTOR. I know you didn't use to.

PATRICK. What's that supposed to mean?

DOCTOR. I'm told you were seen stumbling up the street.

PATRICK. Rubbish. I'm the parson. It's just my bad eyes.

DOCTOR. A dram can improve one's eyesight. Well-known fact.

PATRICK. I've seen the damage drink does to folks. Back in Ireland it was poteen.

DOCTOR. Ah yes, poteen. They make it from barley.

PATRICK. Not barley, potatoes.

DOCTOR. You can't make whisky from spuds.

PATRICK. It's there in the root of the word, pot-een, from pot-atoes.

DOCTOR. Poteen from pot – they distil it in pots.

PATRICK. You've not even been to Ireland.

DOCTOR. You don't even drink.

PATRICK. I don't like the taste.

DOCTOR. I don't like the Irish.

Enter BRANWELL.

BRANWELL. Hey, hey, what's all this?

PATRICK. Something seems to have upset my friend here.

DOCTOR. It was only banter. I meant no harm, Patrick. (*Offers hand.*)

PATRICK (*taking hand*). Me neither. What's the time?

ANNE. Almost nine.

PATRICK. Time I wound the clock and got to bed.

BRANWELL. Good idea. And wear your earplugs: there was a dog howling all last night.

PATRICK. Good idea, son. Now where did I put them?

Exit PATRICK.

ANNE. I didn't hear a dog howling.

BRANWELL. A wolfhound, I think it was.

ANNE. I did hear some noises from down here.

BRANWELL. I sat up with Lydia.

ANNE. Is that what you call it?

BRANWELL. Then I walked her to The Black Bull.

ANNE. You were lucky they'd not locked up.

DOCTOR (*pouring* BRANWELL *a drink*). Here, I know *you'll* have some. Let's make a toast, lad. To your success at the Royal Academy.

BRANWELL. That was years back. I didn't go in the end.

DOCTOR. Well, try another art school.

BRANWELL. There aren't any others.

DOCTOR. Course there are. I know of two at least.

BRANWELL. Who cares how many there are.

DOCTOR. I tell you, there are two art schools in London. There's the Royal Academy and the Royal something else. But you don't have to listen if you won't believe me. Everyone in this house wants to pick a fight with me. I'll not say another word.

Exit DOCTOR.

BRANWELL. What's got into him?

EMILY. What always gets into him: whisky. You encourage it.

BRANWELL. Me?

EMILY. No one else is drinking.

BRANWELL. Is it a sin to have the odd noggin?

EMILY. Drink doesn't agree with you. It makes you wild.

Enter TEACHER.

TEACHER. I thought I should warn you – there's a crowd of men outside. Six or seven of them, carrying weapons, by the look of it. A Chartist mob set on making trouble, I'd say.

EMILY. The Chartists aren't a mob. They're campaigning for the vote.

TEACHER. What do you know about Chartists?

EMILY. Oh, so everything but sewing and cooking is beyond my comprehension, is that it?

TEACHER. They're a bunch of ruffians. Listen to the racket they're making.

Enter TABBY.

TABBY. There's a troupe of musicians at t'door.

TEACHER. Musicians!

TABBY. Aye, they've fiddles and flutes wi' 'em. They've come from T'Black Bull.

EMILY. Tell them they're not wanted, Tabby.

TABBY. Nay, they reckon they were asked.

Pause.

TEACHER. Ah, I see now. How fortuitous I happened to be passing. An evening of madrigals round the hearth. Hymns and ballads to gladden the spirit. The parsonage opening its doors to an array of musical talent and a handful of trusted friends.

ANNE. On a Tuesday night!

EMILY. None of us would ask them at this hour.

ANNE. Not at any hour.

EMILY. Certainly I didn't.

ANNE. Nor me.

BRANWELL. Lydia asked them.

ANNE *and* EMILY. Mrs Robinson?

BRANWELL. As a treat for us all. To provide some entertainment.

EMILY. We make our own entertainment in this house.

ANNE. The noise will keep Father awake.

EMILY. She had no right.

BRANWELL. The doctor will enjoy it.

EMILY. The doctor will enjoy anything in his state.

TEACHER. If I might interject – should the musicians be allowed to play, I'm sure that I too will derive some pleasure from their performance. Spirited fellows they are. Full of vibrancy. I could see that when I passed them in the street.

EMILY. It's our house. And they're not wanted.

ANNE. Tell them we're sorry for any confusion, Tabby.

EMILY. No, we'll speak to them ourselves and explain.

ANNE. And give them some coins for the inconvenience.

Exit EMILY, *ANNE and* TABBY.

TEACHER. Well, what a falling off was there. I'd harboured hopes of an evening in congenial company but how vain are the hopes of men – *o fallacem hominum spem!* In Latin, exclamations always take the accusative. Goodnight.

TEACHER *exits as* DOCTOR *enters*.

DOCTOR. What's happening? I heard a fiddle playing.

BRANWELL. It's nothing, doctor. You imagined it.

DOCTOR. Where have all those girls gone?

BRANWELL. Sit down a second. They'll be back.

DOCTOR. I've always regretted not marrying, you know. I loved your mother, of course. But your father had already taken her, then death took her, so that was that.

BRANWELL. Marriage doesn't bring happiness. Look at Lydia.

DOCTOR. Lydia?

BRANWELL. Mrs Robinson. She's married. Comfortably off, too. But unhappy. Deeply unhappy. All she wants is to be free.

DOCTOR. Freedom's well and good. But what about loneliness? I get so lonely sometimes I could top myself... Ach, enough. What's it matter? What's anything matter? How about a round of whist?

BRANWELL. Not tonight. I promised.

DOCTOR. Promised who? We're not bothering anyone.

BRANWELL. I told Lydia I wouldn't play tonight.

DOCTOR. What's she got to do with it?

BRANWELL. She says I can't play unless she's there. I've no concentration, you see. I've been having these dizzy spells. How can I stop feeling dizzy, doctor?

DOCTOR. Mmm, that's a tricky one... You could try sleeping with your head to the north and passing water every thirty minutes. Otherwise, the best cure's a round of whist.

BRANWELL. I'm going to my room.

Exit BRANWELL.

DOCTOR. There, a fiddle – I knew I'd heard one. What's going on?

Enter ANNE.

ANNE. Some musicians called. But we sent them away. Father needs his sleep. It's nearly my bedtime too. (*Yawns.*)

DOCTOR. I'm sorry, I know I behaved badly tonight. But when a man's in love. And the girl won't even talk to him...

ANNE. Please, don't. It's time you went.

DOCTOR. Your eyes – I've never seen eyes like them.

ANNE. Half-past nine. Did you hear the clock? Sometimes I wonder how it keeps going – the weight of sorrow in this house should have stopped its hands by now.

DOCTOR. And your hair – your lovely hair.

ANNE. Stop it, you're embarrassing me.

DOCTOR. I know I can't force you to love me. But I'll tell you this: if ever another man so much as looks at you, I'll blow his head off.

Enter LYDIA.

LYDIA. Branwell says the musicians have been sent away.

ANNE. It's gone nine. Too late for music.

LYDIA. I thought they'd cheer you up.

ANNE. We're fine – we've things to do.

LYDIA. Such as? Your father's already in bed.

ANNE. Exactly. He goes to bed and... We can't have music disrupting our routine.

DOCTOR. I'd best be off. These girls need their beauty sleep. Can I escort you down the hill, Mrs Robinson?

LYDIA. It's kind of you. But I'm not quite ready.

DOCTOR. Goodnight then.

Exit DOCTOR.

LYDIA. You must be tired.

ANNE. I am.

LYDIA. Me, too. Awfully tired.

ANNE. Shall I get Branwell? He'll walk you down.

LYDIA. It's such a nuisance for him... I was wondering. I meant to ask you earlier... It's just, well, it's so cold and damp at The Black Bull. So I thought, if you didn't mind... Just for a night or two... I brought my luggage with me just in case.

ANNE. What?

LYDIA. If you shared with one of your sisters, then I could have your room.

ANNE. My bedroom, you mean?

LYDIA. It's so... cosy here. Whereas the village is rough. And what if the Chartists start rioting? A woman doesn't feel safe.

ANNE. I suppose I could ask them.

LYDIA. Oh, thank you, you're an angel, you always were. I'll go and tell Branwell.

Exit LYDIA, *enter* CHARLOTTE *and* EMILY.

EMILY. She seems happy.

CHARLOTTE. I thought she'd be gone by now.

ANNE. She asked if she could stop here.

EMILY. We haven't the room.

ANNE. Unless we share. I didn't want to be rude to her, so I said I'd ask you and she...

CHARLOTTE....took it as a yes. It's not decent. People will talk.

EMILY. She *is* married.

ANNE. After a fashion.

EMILY. And Branwell's tutor to her children.

CHARLOTTE. He doesn't behave like a tutor.

EMILY. What do you mean?

CHARLOTTE. It's obvious. Tell her, Anne.

EMILY. What?

ANNE. They're in love.

CHARLOTTE. They're behaving like animals.

ANNE. It started at Thorp Green. Now it's going on here.

CHARLOTTE. He's gambling every night to raise the money to elope with her.

ANNE. But she'll never give up her wealth.

CHARLOTTE. And meanwhile he's squandering the little he has.

EMILY. How do you know all this?

CHARLOTTE. I was in the Post Office. The whole town knows. When Branwell's in his cups he pours his heart out.

EMILY. Poor Branwell.

CHARLOTTE. Poor nothing.

EMILY. He's always been passionate.

CHARLOTTE. His passion's wasted on her.

EMILY. When you feel passion, you've no choice.

CHARLOTTE. He should have chosen to exercise reason, not indulge his baser emotions.

ANNE. Men aren't like us. They're not brought up to resist temptation.

EMILY. We'll cure him of her. I know we can.

CHARLOTTE. I wish I had your confidence.

ANNE. What were you doing in the Post Office anyway?

CHARLOTTE. Sending a package off. Because of this. (*Brandishes letter.*) It came this morning. From London. (*Hands over letter.*) Have a read.

ANNE. For Mr Currer Bell. Was there nothing for Acton or Ellis?

CHARLOTTE. Why would there be? I'm the one looking for a publisher. You two have already found one.

EMILY. 'From Messrs Smith and Elder, 65 Cornhill, London. Dear Mr Bell...'

ANNE. It must be good news.

CHARLOTTE. It is – you'll see.

Enter LYDIA, *in a nightgown*

LYDIA (*embarrassed*). You're still up. I was... looking for a glass of water.

CHARLOTTE. The kitchen's that way.

LYDIA. I'll just tell Branwell he needn't walk me down.

CHARLOTTE. Shall I tell him for you?

LYDIA (*touching nightgown*). This is respectable, surely. (*Sees their look.*) I'll just whisper through his door then.

Exit LYDIA.

CHARLOTTE. Respectable? She doesn't know the meaning of the word.

EMILY (*looking up from letter*). I don't understand – I thought you said it was good news.

ANNE. It's awful. They've turned you down.

CHARLOTTE. Yes, but so courteously I feel more cheered than if they'd accepted me.

ANNE. You must try another publisher.

CHARLOTTE. I've tried six already. No, see what it says at the end – if I've a new book to show them and they like it they'll print it straight away.

ANNE. Well, you have. And of course they'll like it. It's the best thing you've written. You should send it them.

CHARLOTTE. I just have.

ANNE. Good. Then all our books can come out together. And we'll go to London to see our publishers.

EMILY. No we won't.

CHARLOTTE. Let's see.

ANNE (*rapturous*). London!

EMILY (*scornful*). London?

CHARLOTTE (*decisive, nodding*). London.

End of Act Two.

ACT THREE

Morning.

CHARLOTTE. Here, Tabby, help me with these blankets. People might need them.

TABBY. They're saying t'stone bridge on Crow Hill were washed away.

CHARLOTTE. I've never known a storm like it. Father swears he felt the ground move.

TABBY. All t'crops are ruined. And machines in t'mills clogged up wi' mud.

CHARLOTTE. How about food? Should we make soup?

TABBY. Two weavers' cottages in Butt Lane were flattened.

CHARLOTTE. William's lodgings are there. We must send a message. He and his sister can stay here.

TABBY. We're packed to t'rafters as it is.

CHARLOTTE. Perhaps the doctor will take them. Though he'll be busy, of course…

TABBY. T'doctor's not busy, he's drunk.

CHARLOTTE. Oh, he would be when he's needed. I sometimes think he does it on purpose. No, the two of them will have to stay here.

TABBY. Don't send me away, miss.

CHARLOTTE. No one's sending you away, Tabby.

TABBY. I've buttery fingers and wobbly pins, but I do my best. Where else can I go?

CHARLOTTE. You're not going anywhere. There's room in the house for all of us. You rest a while. You look pale.

Enter LYDIA.

LYDIA. What a fuss everyone's making. You'd think it was Noah's Flood, not a little thunderstorm.

CHARLOTTE. Tons of mud have washed down from the moor.

LYDIA. Well, yes, it's jolly inconvenient. But...

CHARLOTTE. People have lost their homes. We must start a fund for the victims.

LYDIA. Well, I'll be generous, of course; I always am; one must remember the less fortunate. (*Seeing blankets.*) So long as none of them actually crosses the threshold. Goodness knows what diseases they're carrying. It's not myself I worry about. It's my children. What if I infect them when I return home?

CHARLOTTE (*not listening*). The beck was a torrent.

LYDIA. Look at me: is that a grey hair? Branwell says I'm putting on weight. It's not true, my waist is as slender as it ever was.

TABBY. Rain's easing off now, miss.

LYDIA. He was always so gracious at Thorp Green. Now he's here, his manners have deserted him. Oh, he's attentive, I will say that. But a woman ought to be treated with dignity, not slobbered over like a bone.

TABBY. And t'beck's not so full.

LYDIA. A pot of tea would be nice. (*To* TABBY.) Did you hear, *tea*? Don't just stand there when I'm talking to you. Go on, move.

TABBY *gets up and exits.*

I can't understand why you keep her on.

CHARLOTTE. And I can't understand your manner. In this house we don't speak like that.

LYDIA. If she were working for a farmer's wife, it might be tolerated. But here, in a parsonage, among educated people... You spoil her, Charlotte. (*Softening.*) Oh, I know you're tired from all this school business. There's nowhere available, I hear. It must be so disheartening.

CHARLOTTE. We're considering having the school in the house. Once Branwell's back tutoring your children, and we've some rooms spare... But it all costs money. And Anne and Emily are so frail. Have you heard them coughing?... You were very unkind to Tabby just now.

LYDIA. It's the only language servants understand.

CHARLOTTE. Perhaps Father has brought us up the wrong way. But to hear you speak like that makes me ill.

LYDIA. I'm sorry. But she just sits and sleeps and potters about.

CHARLOTTE. She does the washing. She lays the grate. She peels the potatoes...

LYDIA. And leaves the eyes in them.

CHARLOTTE. Because her own eyes are failing.

LYDIA. Exactly.

CHARLOTTE. She's nearly eighty. We really don't mind.

LYDIA. At Thorp Green I have a cook, a gardener, a nurse, a chambermaid, a coachman, a tutor – ten servants in all. The slightest hint of slovenliness or impertinence and I dismiss them. How anyone manages with just a housekeeper I can't imagine. No wonder it's rather... dingy in here. I could find you a new housekeeper tomorrow.

Enter TABBY; LYDIA *lowers her voice.*

Your poor father deserves better. Why *won't* you let me? You're so stubborn, Charlotte. Only one cup, Tabby? What about Branwell? Oh, he can have mine.

Exit LYDIA, *exasperated.*

TABBY. Doctor's on his way through, miss.

CHARLOTTE. He ought to be in town, helping.

TABBY. He's stewed as a prune, like I said.

CHARLOTTE. *I* don't want to see him. Quick...

Exit TABBY *and* CHARLOTTE; *enter* DOCTOR.

DOCTOR. People think because I'm a doctor I'm God. But there's nothing I can do to help people. Or if there is I've forgotten it. Last week I saw a woman in Oxenhope. She'd bad diarrhoea and was running a fever. Just a touch of flu, I told her husband. Next day he was weeping over her corpse. Not flu, cholera. Twenty years back I'd have diagnosed it. Now my head's an empty shell. Maybe all of me's a shell, and I don't exist at all – so when I walk or wave my hand or eat fried eggs I'm only imagining it. I might as well be dead. The other night here they were talking about Milton and Shakespeare. I've not read a word of them but of course I pretended I had. Then in the middle of their blathering I thought of that woman in Oxenhope. That's when I started drinking again. (*Slumps in chair with hip flask.*)

Enter ANNE *and* CURATE.

ANNE. I'm sure Emily's here somewhere.

CURATE. Not to worry. It was *you* I wanted to see.

ANNE. Me?

CURATE. Yes – to make sure you'd come to no harm. (*Reaches for her hand.*) Did you heard the thunderclap? And see the lightning? It was just like Pentecost. A rushing wind then tongues of flame. Your father thinks it's a punishment from God. He's down there preaching already: 'Unless those of you mired in sin mend your ways, the earth shall tremble and dissolve.' You're sure you're all right? Our house wasn't affected. My sister slept right through it. I did worry for you. You were my first thought, in fact. How's dear Anne, I wondered.

DOCTOR *makes a noise.*

ANNE. I didn't see you there, doctor. You look... tired.

DOCTOR. I'm fine.

CURATE. More than fine, I'd say. Don't they need you in town?

DOCTOR. Me? No. There's just a few suffering from exposure, nothing serious. I had an idea, though. To raise money for those who've lost their homes. A concert. We must have a piano concert.

ANNE. Excellent. But who'd play?

DOCTOR. You'd play.

ANNE. You'd be better asking Emily. I play so badly.

DOCTOR. Nonsense. I know about music. And I can tell you, you play beautifully.

ANNE. We heard Paganini once, in Halifax. That's proper music.

CURATE. Of course, your father would have to approve. Only *sacred* music would be fitting.

DOCTOR. I'll talk to Patrick, just leave it to me. (*Picks up an ornament and examines it.*)

CURATE. Your father's warning people to expect an inferno next time: 'Let the ungodly repent before God consumes them with fire.'

ANNE. Fire terrifies him. He won't let us have curtains in the house in case a candle sets them alight… Sometimes I feel there's already been a fire – that's why everything in the house looks black and charred.

CURATE. Except the occupants: you look pure and untouched.

ANNE (*embarrassed*). How is Father?

CURATE. In his element. I left him to it. The people here are really his flock, not mine.

ANNE. He values you so much. We all do.

CURATE. I'm just his curate. My role is secondary. Soon I'll have to move on.

ANNE. Not for ages, I hope.

CURATE. I don't want to go. Not now I've reasons for staying – personal reasons, close to the heart. But I may have to.

ANNE. You mustn't. We'd miss you so much.

   Crash of ornament as DOCTOR *drops it.*

DOCTOR. How did that happen?

ANNE. That was Mother's.

DOCTOR. Then it was precious, and I'm sorry. But perhaps I didn't smash it.

CURATE. You did. We saw.

DOCTOR. Perhaps it only appears that I did. Just as it only appears that the three of us are in this room together, when in reality we don't exist at all. I'm no philosopher, but it seems to me that none of us can be sure of anything any more. Stop looking at me as though I'm drunk. I know what I'm talking about. I know about Branwell and Mrs Robinson. And I know about you two – he's been flirting with you and you're hooked. So excuse me before I do something I'd regret.

Exit DOCTOR.

CURATE. What was that about?

ANNE (*embarrassed*). I'm sorry, take no notice. When he's sober, we all love him. But when he drinks, we despair... You were saying, about leaving – Father's eyes are bad, he does need a curate.

CURATE. It's my sister. Her mind's not right. I worry what she'll do to herself if I don't get her away. Forgive me, I've never talked about this to anyone. It's odd how easy I feel in your presence. You're the only person I dare be honest with. (*Clasps her hand.*) You're not angry with me, are you? I do love your eyes. What colour are they? Dark grey, dark blue? There's a kindling to them, a glow, as if they were burning coals...

ANNE. Stop! When you talk like that, it makes me nervous. Well, you don't have to stop altogether, just... (*Lowers her head.*) If I don't look at you I can pretend you're talking to someone else...

CURATE. That's no good. I can't see your eyes now. Come closer. (*Grabs her hand again.*) Look at me.

Enter EMILY.

ANNE (*embarrassed*). Emily! Where've you sprung from?

EMILY. I was dozing in the kitchen. The doctor woke me. He says he's giving up medicine and getting a job at the brickworks.

CURATE. Anne's inspired him: work, work, work.

EMILY. He's in love with Anne, that's the problem.

ANNE. He's a silly old man.

CURATE. And a drunk.

EMILY. No he's serious: *amo, amas, amat, amamus, amatis, amant*.

ANNE. Don't talk about love.

EMILY. I won't. The word's like a nail being hammered through my head. The lovesick curate: bang, bang, bang.

CURATE. Is that your father coming in? I'll see how he is.

Exit CURATE*; awkward silence between the two sisters*.

ANNE. Has something upset you?

EMILY. Yes. Badly. (*Pause*.) Branwell. Since Mrs Robinson came, he barely speaks to me.

ANNE. She's all he can think about. It was the same at Thorp Green.

EMILY Remember the ambitions he used to have. Those poems he wrote.

ANNE. And sent to Mr Wordsworth.

EMILY. And when he painted.

ANNE. And belonged to the Temperance Society.

EMILY. And worked as a railway clerk in Sowerby Bridge.

ANNE. He was going to be Mayor of Bradford, he said.

EMILY. He could still do something with his life. If Mrs Robinson went. I wish she would, before his heart's broken.

Enter CHARLOTTE.

CHARLOTTE. Whose heart's broken?

EMILY. No one's.

ANNE. We were talking about Branwell. Being in love is destroying him.

CHARLOTTE. It's not love.

EMILY. He thinks it is.

CHARLOTTE. He's making a fool of himself.

ANNE. Is that what love does – make you mad? I used to think it made you happy. Remember those stories we wrote as children, about dukes and knights and queens and princesses, and everyone being brave and independent and finding true love. Maybe you never believed in that world but I did. I thought I'd even live in it one day. Now I feel stupid.

CHARLOTTE. It's not stupid to believe in love. *Real* love.

ANNE. Oh, I love my family – you, and Emily, and Father, and Tabby, and Branwell. But that's not the same as falling in love.

CHARLOTTE. You're still young. It'll happen one day. There are hundreds of good men in the world.

ANNE. But ten to one I'll never meet them or, if I do, twenty to one against them being single or taking a fancy to me.

CHARLOTTE. The doctor's a good man.

ANNE. I wasn't thinking of the doctor.

CHARLOTTE. I know he's much older than you…

ANNE. And he's drunk all the time.

CHARLOTTE. He's only drinking because he's miserable. If he thought you'd marry him, he'd stop.

ANNE. Marry him! You don't even *believe* in marriage.

CHARLOTTE. It's different for me. I'm like a toad in a block of marble. You're young.

ANNE. Naive, you mean. What if men like those in our stories don't exist? Or if you fall in love with someone who's not good? Or if a man you think you could love says he loves you, or doesn't say it but makes you *feel* he loves you – what are you meant to do then? I don't understand about love.

CHARLOTTE. You'll understand when you experience it.

ANNE. How do you know? What do *you* know about love?

CHARLOTTE (*angry*). You think I don't have feelings, that I'm an automaton. But I did love a man once, in Brussels.

ANNE. I know. It's sad.

CHARLOTTE. I hoped he would write to me, anything, crumbs would have done. I still keep hoping. But he never does.

ANNE. He's a married man. He has his wife to think of.

EMILY *whistles*.

CHARLOTTE. Of course. Brussels was a selfish folly and I've been punished for it. But I'll not pine away. I'm my own woman now, free to do good and help others.

EMILY. Doing good and helping others! That's what people expect of single women. But where's the happiness in denying ourselves? Where's the passion? If that's all life holds, then make an end of me now. I don't want to walk about for ten years like a dead woman.

CHARLOTTE. All I'm saying is that marriage isn't for me. But it might be for Anne.

EMILY. Not unless she's passionate about someone.

CHARLOTTE. Passion rarely lasts beyond the honeymoon. It's better to marry *to* love than to marry *for* love. Respect someone and love will follow.

ANNE. I couldn't respect the doctor. But perhaps someone else…

CHARLOTTE. Let your eyes be blind to external charms and your ears deaf to flattery. Marriage is a solemn business.

ANNE. But if I merely approve of a man, rather than love him… What do you think, Emily?

EMILY. I'll never marry a man unless there's passion.

LYDIA *passes through, half-dressed, with a bag in her hand.*

ANNE. No need to ask where she's been.

CHARLOTTE. Under our roof. It's disgusting.

EMILY. It's life. It's passion. People have bodies.

CHARLOTTE. That's no excuse. You really do say the stupidest things.

Pause.

EMILY. Well, here's another stupid thing. I'll never confess it to anyone else, only you two, this once. (*Sotto voce.*) It's a secret, like our pseudonyms. Well, then. I do know about love…

ANNE. You're in love with William, it's obvious.

CHARLOTTE. I knew it. I don't want to hear.

EMILY. You're jealous. It's you who're in love with him.

CHARLOTTE. He's a flirt, Emily. He sweet-talks every woman he sees.

EMILY. I know that. When I walked in just now, he was doing it to Anne – *and* succeeding.

ANNE. He did it to you too.

EMILY. We all thought he was comical at first – his voice, his hands, the way he talks about his sister.

CHARLOTTE. If he has a sister – we've never even seen her. You think he'd do something better than fritter his time away on three spinsters.

EMILY. I agree. But I wasn't talking about William.

ANNE. Who then?

EMILY. No one. No man I've ever met in the flesh. But I can picture him, I can see his face, I can even imagine myself saying 'I love you'. 'I love you': how sentimental that seems when you read it in a book. But it's the deepest feeling. And as for controlling love – well, you might as well try fitting the sea inside a horse trough. Oh, I know you think I'm inventing all this but I can feel it, and when I do fall in love it won't be with a man like William. No, he'll be darker and stranger, like a twisted mirror image, someone more myself than I am, and I'll love him not from choice or through pleasure, but because he's inside me, like my own being. Yes, it's a dream, but the dream has gone through me like wine through water and the world's a different colour now. There, I've finished. I'll not say another word about it.

Enter TABBY *and* BRANWELL (*half-dressed*).

BRANWELL. What are you on about? I don't understand.

TABBY. Some men are outside. On account of t'bog-burst. They're asking will t'parson let 'em use t'gravestones to dry their bedding on.

BRANWELL. Am *I* the parson? It's my father they want.

TABBY. Your dad's not here. You're t'only Mr Brontë they can ask.

BRANWELL. All right, all right, but tell them it's just for today, we can't have them making a habit of it.

TABBY. There's a coachman come and all.

BRANWELL. Oh, be off with you. What do I care?

Exit TABBY.

It's one interruption after another. I'm going to have a wash and get dressed. I promised to take Lydia to Bolton Abbey, if it stops raining. (*Calls offstage.*) Tabby! (*To his sisters.*) Tell her to fetch me a bowl of warm water, will you. Oh, and this came for you, Charlotte. You've been getting a lot of these, haven't you. (*Hands* CHARLOTTE *a letter.*) 'Mr Currer Bell, c/o Miss C. Brontë': what's *that* about?

Exit BRANWELL.

EMILY. He knows something. You've not mentioned our books to him?

ANNE. Of course not.

CHARLOTTE. He might suspect but he *can't* know, no one does. (*Opens letter.*)

EMILY. He'll be mad with jealousy if he finds out.

ANNE. I always thought he'd be the one to have a book out.

EMILY. So did I.

CHARLOTTE. So did he.

LYDIA (*voice offstage*). Tabby!

BRANWELL (*voice offstage*). Tabby!

Enter TABBY. *The voices continue calling. Torn between them, she finally heads towards* LYDIA. *Exit* TABBY.

EMILY. Tabby knows who's boss round here.

ANNE (*laughs*). What's in the letter, Charlotte?

CHARLOTTE. Oh, it's a muddle. My publishers think we're all one person.

ANNE. What?

CHARLOTTE. There's a rumour our three books came from a single hand. That Currer, Ellis and Acton are the same man. My publishers are very angry – they think I've deceived them by publishing two other books – your books – with a rival company. This could ruin my career before it's even started.

ANNE. We've done nothing wrong.

CHARLOTTE. Except use pseudonyms.

EMILY. That's not illegal.

CHARLOTTE. No, but they want the truth.

ANNE. What can we do?

CHARLOTTE. We'll have to visit them in London. And show them there really are three of us.

EMILY. They'll see we're women if we do.

ANNE. We never said we were men.

EMILY. But they assume we are. They'd not publish us otherwise. If the names on our books were women's names, we'd be sure to get horrible reviews.

CHARLOTTE. Or reviews that flatter us out of gallantry and make our books sound novelettish.

EMILY. I'm Ellis Bell and I'm staying Ellis Bell.

CHARLOTTE. But we still have to go to London and explain.

EMILY. I'm not going.

ANNE. We'll go without you, then.

EMILY. And rob me of my privacy.

CHARLOTTE. No, we'll not say a thing. You can stay Ellis. All they need to know is there are three different writers.

EMILY. You should never have let them send letters here. I swear Branwell's got wind of it.

CHARLOTTE. All the more reason to go. If we don't stop the rumours, he'll claim that *he* wrote our books.

ANNE. When should we leave?

CHARLOTTE. As soon as we can.

Enter LYDIA, *fully dressed, with* TABBY *behind her carrying luggage.*

LYDIA. You can have your room back now, Anne. Have you thought of redecorating it? A shade of pink would cheer it up. I have to go, I'm afraid. My coachman's waiting outside. He says my children have missed me terribly. Such dear children. Where would one be without children? The graveyard's so gloomy. You should think of planting some trees. I've suggested it to your father but he takes no notice – with his eyes, it makes no difference, I suppose. (*To* ANNE.) You'd look prettier in blue or green, my dear. Grey's so unfashionable. Something floral, perhaps. And this room could do with *real* flowers. Tabby, you must buy some from the market this morning. Say goodbye to Branwell for me – I don't want to disturb him. Tell him to write to me once I'm home again. Who left this fork lying round? Honestly, Tabby! Goodbye, everyone. It's been a pleasure. You will tell your father what I said about the trees?

Exit LYDIA *and* TABBY.

ANNE. See, I'd a hunch she was leaving.

EMILY. Good riddance.

CHARLOTTE. 'Where would one be without children?' As if she cares a fig about hers. A worse mother, a worse woman, doesn't exist.

ANNE. How gracious of her to give me my room back.

CHARLOTTE. The rich aren't like us – they've no morality, they see everything the wrong way up.

EMILY. Say goodbye to Branwell for her – did she not tell him she was leaving?

ANNE. She must have. Surely.

CHARLOTTE. Maybe her husband's summoned her.

ANNE. Or the accommodation didn't meet her standards.

EMILY. She's gone, that's all that matters. We can start to take Branwell in hand.

BRANWELL (*offstage*). Lydia? Lydia! (*Enters, scruffy but dressed.*) Where's Lydia? (*Looks at them.*) Well?

End of Act Three.

ACT FOUR

In an echo of the opening to Act One, EMILY *is circling the table in semi-darkness, anxious and perturbed.*

CHARLOTTE *and* ANNE *appear from the rear, put their bags down, take their coats off and join her. Lights come up to catch them in mid-conversation.*

ANNE. First we had to walk through a downpour to Keighley. Then we got the train to Leeds. Then first class on the night train to London. When we arrived we went straight to our lodgings, had a wash, had breakfast, sat for a few minutes, then set off for Cornhill. I was half out of my mind with excitement.

CHARLOTTE. You were terrified.

ANNE. My nerves were like catgut. Stretched to breaking point.

CHARLOTTE. Smith & Elder's is also a bookshop. So we went to the counter and asked for Mr Smith. The lad seemed surprised – two frumpy women with northern accents wanting his boss – but he went to fetch him. Then he came back on his own saying Mr Smith wanted to know our names.

ANNE. We could have said Bell, but all we said was, it was private. So the lad went off again. Then this tall youngish gentleman appeared from the back of the shop. 'Did you wish to see me?' he said. 'Is it Mr Smith?' Charlotte said. 'It is indeed,' he said. Then Charlotte handed him his letter.

CHARLOTTE. The one he'd just sent me, addressed to Currer Bell.

ANNE. 'Where'd you get this?' he said, and stared at us, baffled, and looked at the letter, and looked at us, and then it dawned on him and we all smiled.

EMILY. *What* dawned? What did you tell him?

CHARLOTTE. We didn't say anything... not then.

ANNE. But we knew he knew. He took us to a back room, and introduced us to Mr Williams, who's older, about fifty, and we chatted, or *they* chatted, and Mr Smith said we must stay a few days and meet his two sisters, and if Mr Thackeray was in town maybe we'd like to meet him too, because he'd read our books and admired us and...

EMILY. But what did you say about our names?

ANNE. Well, Charlotte stopped him then, you see, and went all serious, and told him straight.

CHARLOTTE. 'We are three sisters,' I said.

EMILY. Three! So he knows there's no Ellis. How could you?

CHARLOTTE. I'm sorry. It just slipped out.

EMILY. You betrayed me, Charlotte.

ANNE. We made him swear never to use your name, even in letters. Nor to tell another soul. Only he and Mr Williams know...

EMILY.... And Mr Thackeray and half of London.

CHARLOTTE. We were invited to meet Mr Thackeray. Mr Smith said he'd pass us off as country cousins. But we decided the risk was too great.

ANNE. We didn't want him making a show of us, either.

CHARLOTTE. *And* I had a bad headache. So we said we had to get back home

EMILY. That was Saturday. It's Tuesday now.

ANNE. Well, in the end Mr Smith persuaded us to stay, you see. We went to the opera. *The Barber of Seville*.

CHARLOTTE. We weren't dressed for it – I could see these fancy ladies looking down their noses at us. But Mr Smith had bought tickets.

ANNE. We didn't get to bed till after one. Then next morning we went to church. And on Sunday night we had dinner at the Smiths'.

EMILY. Dinner?

ANNE. An evening meal. Supper. Then on Monday we visited the Royal Academy.

CHARLOTTE. And the National Gallery.

ANNE. And then had supper at the Smiths' again.

CHARLOTTE. And then this morning we left. With all these books Mr Smith gave us. There's one for you, look, Mr Tennyson's *Poems*.

EMILY. Signed 'To Emily', I suppose.

CHARLOTTE. No, the publishers gave us their word. No one else knows. You'd like them – they're kind. When I mentioned your cough to Mr Williams, he gave me this homeopathic remedy...

EMILY. Homeopathy's for quacks. I don't need his remedies.

CHARLOTTE. You're impossible, Emily. He's trying to help.

ANNE. We bought some new gloves, look, and three parasols. The trip cost a small fortune.

CHARLOTTE. Fourteen pounds in all.

ANNE. It was worth it, though. I've seen London now. Not that I liked it that much – there's more smoke and dirt than in Bradford.

CHARLOTTE. Anne was coughing a lot.

ANNE. I'm glad to be back. What's been happening?

EMILY (*shifty*). Nothing much... William came round, hoping to see you.

ANNE. Me?

EMILY. You're the one he's sweet on.

ANNE. He likes you too.

CHARLOTTE. He likes all women.

EMILY. He's leaving soon, anyway. That's what he came to say.

ANNE. Oh... What will Father do? He needs William – he's nearly blind.

CHARLOTTE. They can fix cataracts these days. I'm going to get him to Manchester for the operation.

Enter TABBY.

Tabby! Are you not in bed at this hour?

TABBY. I were in bed. Till I smelled smoke.

ANNE. It's these clothes. London's so smoggy.

TABBY. Nay, it's not you, it's Branwell. He came in drunk half an hour since. And now there's smoke pouring under his door. I reckon he's set fire to his bed.

ANNE. I'll come with you.

Exit ANNE *with* TABBY.

CHARLOTTE. Has he been drinking since we left?

EMILY. He's upset.

CHARLOTTE. Any excuse will do.

EMILY. No, but he *is* upset. Mr Robinson sent a letter. He's dismissed as tutor. Banned from any further contact with the family. And if he ever tries to see Lydia again, he'll be shot.

CHARLOTTE. A married woman... what did he expect?

EMILY. He's been beside himself. When I came in this morning he was waving Father's pistol around – I had to take it off him.

CHARLOTTE. Where's it now?

EMILY (*points to wooden chest*). Back in the chest.

CHARLOTTE What's that doing here? Father keeps it in his study.

EMILY. He had some bills to pay.

CHARLOTTE. Branwell's, you mean.

EMILY. A sheriff's officer came from York. He was going to cart Branwell off to jail. Father had to settle up for him.

CHARLOTTE. He's been screwing money out of Father for years.

EMILY. You know how Father dotes on him.

CHARLOTTE (*riffling through chest*). There used to be banknotes in here, now it's just promissory notes. 'I owe ten pounds, to be repaid tomorrow.' 'I owe fifteen pounds, to be repaid next month.' 'I owe twenty pounds…' – to be repaid never. Half Father's savings are gone.

EMILY. I'm sure Branwell asked his permission.

CHARLOTTE. I'm sure he didn't. I'm locking this and taking the key.

EMILY. We can earn the money back, so Father never knows.

CHARLOTTE. You're always covering up for Branwell.

EMILY. There's the shares we bought in the railways – they must be worth something. And if we get the school started, we'll get fees from that. And maybe our books will sell.

CHARLOTTE. It's not right. We shouldn't have to.

Enter ANNE, *with a burned sheet and several empty bottles*.

ANNE. It's lucky Tabby was awake. He'd have gone up in smoke otherwise.

CHARLOTTE. It might be better if he did.

EMILY. How can you say that?

CHARLOTTE. All he's good for is grief and debauchery.

EMILY. He's still our brother. (*To* ANNE.) Where's he now?

ANNE. In his room, flat-out.

EMILY. He'll be down in a minute, wanting a drink.

CHARLOTTE. The pub's shut.

EMILY. He's a stash of bottles in the house.

CHARLOTTE. Where?

EMILY. I don't know – he hides them all over.

They search for bottles. CHARLOTTE *finds one. Enter* BRANWELL, *drunk.*

BRANWELL. Ah, my three sisters, conspiring against me as usual. Give me that, Charlotte. I hear you've been to London.

CHARLOTTE. On a business matter, yes.

BRANWELL (*parroting*). 'On a business matter.' Since when do the daughters of a country clergyman have business to conduct in London? Go on, give it me.

CHARLOTTE. You've drunk too much already.

BRANWELL. That's *my* business.

CHARLOTTE. I know you feel disconsolate…

BRANWELL. Dis-con-so-late. Never.

CHARLOTTE. And perhaps it seems unjust to you…

BRANWELL. What?

CHARLOTTE. But you can hardly blame Mr Robinson.

BRANWELL. I don't know what you're talking about.

CHARLOTTE. I'm sure you do.

BRANWELL. You'd think I was your enemy, the way you talk.

CHARLOTTE. It's been a long day, Branwell.

BRANWELL. My own sisters, ranged against me.

CHARLOTTE. The journey took ten hours. We're exhausted.

EMILY. We're on your side, Branwell. Just leave it till morning.

CHARLOTTE. Emily's right. We'll talk about it tomorrow.

She makes to leave, but BRANWELL *stops her.*

BRANWELL. Well, I've something to say even if you've not. First off, I don't like your attitude to Lydia. Oh, I know you've a grudge against her, because she's rich and wears fine clothes. But she's all I could wish for in a woman and she loves me even better than I love her. As you've doubtless been told, I'll not be returning to tutor her children, I've quit the post by mutual agreement. But our feelings for each other haven't altered. Once her husband dies, Lydia and I will be wed. So I expect you to treat her with respect. Point two: you seem to think I've been idling my time away. But I've not, I still write poems, and I'll be sending them off to be published soon, and then the world can acclaim me: Branwell Brontë, poet, genius, Brother Superior. Meanwhile, thirdly: I will take up paid employment. I'm contemplating a return to the railways – there's a new line being proposed from Hebden Bridge to Keighley, and they're in need of a Secretary, a man of education and refinement. Fourth… well, I have run up a debt or two of late, as you know, and Father has had to help me out, but any loans are only temporary. Bear in mind that Lydia's a wealthy woman who wants the best for me… So, to sum up: I deserve some respect from you. Once I'm married, and a rich man in a big house, we'll be set up nicely, you and all. Right? Right? Don't you believe me?

CHARLOTTE. How can we? Even you don't believe it.

BRANWELL. You're pinched, Charlotte, you're cold and puritanical. You all are. Weak and shrivelled and mean-minded. That's why I love Lydia. She knows what a man needs. Whereas you know nothing of men, nothing of life, nothing of love, nothing worth knowing at all. I'll have that, thanks.

Exit BRANWELL *with bottle.*

ANNE. 'They knew nothing of life': it sounds like an epitaph.

EMILY. He didn't mean it. By tomorrow he'll have forgotten he said it.

ANNE. I won't.

CHARLOTTE. We should go to bed.

ANNE. I couldn't sleep after that.

EMILY. Let's read to each other.

CHARLOTTE. Good idea. Do you have something, Emily?

EMILY. There's Mr Tennyson's *Poems*.

ANNE. No, something by you.

EMILY. I've not written anything for months. I've given up.

ANNE. You mustn't. You've a gift.

CHARLOTTE. Yes, just keep going.

ANNE. If Emily won't read, I will. It's a poem.

> 'Why should such gloomy silence reign;
> And why is all the house so drear,
> When neither danger, sickness, pain,
> Nor death nor want have entered here?
> We are as many as we were
> That other night, when all were gay,
> And full of hope, and free from care;
> Yet is there something gone away...'

Lights fade as they circle the table, with ANNE *reading.*

End of Act Four.

ACT FIVE

Day.

PATRICK. Isn't it grand. Everyone's leaving at once – the doctor, the teacher, the curate. We'll have some peace at last.

CHARLOTTE. We'll feel bereft.

PATRICK. Not me. The teacher's a pedant, the doctor's useless at chess, and the curate talks too much. It'll be different with the next curate.

CHARLOTTE. The *next* curate? Lord preserve us.

PATRICK. I need help, my dear.

CHARLOTTE. Nonsense. Your eyes are fine now.

PATRICK. There's still too much work for one man. And I've the perfect candidate. An Irishman. Dr Arthur Nicholls. Ugly as a bulldog and dour as a drainpipe. Just what's wanted.

CHARLOTTE. I'm sure I'll hate him.

PATRICK. I'm sure you won't.

CHARLOTTE. It's a pity the doctor's going. He has a soft spot for Anne, you know.

PATRICK. He's a silly old fool.

CHARLOTTE. I'd not be surprised if he asks her to marry him…

PATRICK. She's too young.

CHARLOTTE. Not that young.

PATRICK. He's quite unsuitable.

CHARLOTTE. Every man's unsuitable in your eyes, Father.

PATRICK. I didn't educate you to marry old drunks or yapping curates. You're better off stopping here, with me. So long as there's food on the table and needlework to occupy you, what more do you need?

CHARLOTTE. There is one thing.

PATRICK. What's that, pray?

CHARLOTTE. Books. We couldn't live without books.

PATRICK. True enough. We're all readers in this house.

CHARLOTTE. Not just readers. Every night when you're in bed, we write.

PATRICK. Oh, I know you're always writing letters...

CHARLOTTE. Not just letters. Stories. Poems...

PATRICK. I was a bit of a poet myself, in my youth.

CHARLOTTE. What I'm trying to say is that I've written a book.

PATRICK. Have you, my dear?

CHARLOTTE. Yes, and I'd like you to read it. (*Hands him book.*)

PATRICK. I can't – it'll be wasted on me.

CHARLOTTE. But your eyesight's good now. You said it yourself.

PATRICK. Even so, I can never make out your writing.

CHARLOTTE. It's not a manuscript. It's printed.

PATRICK. But the cost! How could you afford it?

CHARLOTTE. I didn't pay for it to be printed, a publisher did.

PATRICK. They must be daft. Nobody's heard of you.

CHARLOTTE. I've chosen a different name, Currer Bell, see.

PATRICK. What good will that do? No one's heard of him, either.

CHARLOTTE. No. But the book seems to be selling. I've brought you some reviews.

PATRICK. All right, I'll try a page or two. But you mustn't forget your duties. Books can't be the business of a woman's life.

CHARLOTTE. Of course not, Father.

Enter TEACHER.

PATRICK. So you're on your way?

TEACHER. Indeed so. I've come to offer my parting felicitations.

PATRICK. Goodbye then – we'll probably never meet again.

TEACHER. Don't say that. I've still some hope of persuading your daughters to come and work for me.

CHARLOTTE. There's little chance of that, I'm afraid.

TEACHER. Still planning to start your own school, eh?

CHARLOTTE. No, we've dropped that idea. But I've come into a little income of late. I was just telling Father.

TEACHER. That investment in the railways, is it?

CHARLOTTE. Not exactly. But something else we've been investing in has come good.

TEACHER. Well, there'll always be a post for you when the money runs out. A good mistress is hard to find.

CHARLOTTE. So I'm told... We heard there was some sort of set-to last night. Between the doctor and the curate.

TEACHER. Yes, I heard that. Just a few words exchanged, I believe.

CHARLOTTE. Nothing to worry about, then.

TEACHER. I shouldn't think it will be 'pistols at dawn', no... Anyway, I mustn't leave without giving your father a present. This is for you, sir. A little book I've written, about the school here. The name of every pupil is recorded, see. There's some light relief, too, in the anecdotes I tell – schoolboy howlers and such. Children still have such trouble with Latin. I remember a boy when I was at school called Cosgrove. He's working as a cobbler now, because they expelled him at fifteen for not knowing his ablatives. 'Hello, Ablative,' I say, whenever I run into him. Poor old Cosgrove. Whereas I've been lucky all my life. The Halifax diocese recently commended me, you know – the diploma of St Xavier, second class, for services in the teaching of Latin. Yes, I still know my vocatives from my locatives. I'm clever, of course, cleverer than most people. But being clever doesn't make you happy, I'm not saying that.

Enter ANNE.

PATRICK. Ah, my little sparrow – I'll let you say your goodbyes to Mr Rand. I've been given two books today. I must go and read them.

Exit PATRICK.

TEACHER. I trust it's only temporary, this parting of the ways. I'm not going far – only Stalybridge.

ANNE. I already feel lonely. The doctor is considering some practices down south and he offered to take me to London. But I've been there now. Just the other week. Charlotte and I caught the train down...

CHARLOTTE. For a private business matter.

ANNE. We had a good trip. But I'll not go back. My place is here now.

TEACHER. Well, remember, there's always an opening for you as my mistress...

ANNE. That's kind... (*Seeing* DOCTOR *arrive.*) Come through and see Tabby. You mustn't leave without one of her cakes.

TEACHER. Excellent idea.

Exit TEACHER *and* ANNE; *enter* DOCTOR.

CHARLOTTE. So you really are going. I never thought you would.

DOCTOR. There's too much work here. I used to pretend to take my duties lightly. But then one day I counted up all the people I'd treated, all the diseases I'd seen, all the children whose fading pulse I'd held. It wasn't that I'd lost my skills, just that I'd too many patients. And, of course, I was drinking too much. Now I'm ready for a fresh start. A small rural practice in the south. Where I won't be ground down.

CHARLOTTE. I remember when you treated us as children. Tell me honestly: were you in love with our mother?

DOCTOR. I suppose I was.

CHARLOTTE. Did she love you?

DOCTOR. I doubt she ever considered it. She loved your father. And she was busy having children.

CHARLOTTE. When you look at Anne, do you see our mother in her?

DOCTOR. I see a lovely young woman.

CHARLOTTE. Whereas Emily and I are ugly and crabby.

DOCTOR. Not at all.

CHARLOTTE. Emily worries me. She barely leaves the house these days.

DOCTOR. Would you like me to listen to her chest?

CHARLOTTE. I don't think she's ill. But there's something burning inside her, and there's nowhere for it to go. She's like a pan on a stove, boiling and boiling.

Enter BRANWELL, *distracted.*

Branwell's the same, only worse. He's boiled over and boiled dry.

BRANWELL. Have any letters come?

CHARLOTTE. I don't think so. Why?

BRANWELL. Mr Robinson's dead. It was in the paper. They had the funeral last week. I've been waiting for Lydia to write. Maybe I should just turn up on her.

CHARLOTTE. I'm sure if she wants you there, she'll send word.

BRANWELL. All her relations are against me.

CHARLOTTE. If she cares enough, that won't stop her.

BRANWELL. Of course she cares.

CHARLOTTE (*exasperated*). I'm going to help Tabby.

Exit CHARLOTTE.

DOCTOR. So what are you going to do?

BRANWELL. Get wed as soon as we can. She once told me I was the man of her dreams. And I feel the same about her. Only... Perhaps you understand this, doctor, for all her refinement there's something very narrow about Lydia. She's no interests other than clothes and jewellery. And she never reads books.

DOCTOR. If you want my advice, you'll forget all about her. Pack a bag, take yourself off somewhere and don't look back. The further away, the better.

BRANWELL. You don't understand. I might not approve of Lydia, but I love her.

Enter TABBY.

TABBY. There's a man wants to see you. He'll be waiting at T'Black Bull

BRANWELL. If I owe him money, he's wasting his time.

TABBY. He's come all t'way from York.

BRANWELL. Not the sheriff's officer again. What did he say?

TABBY. Just that roads over t'tops were riddled with potholes. And that he in't looking forrad to t'journey back.

BRANWELL. What's his name?

TABBY. Allan Willis or summat.

BRANWELL. Allison, William Allison.

TABBY. Aye, that's it.

BRANWELL. She's sent him to fetch me. I knew she would. Oh, this is wonderful. Lydia's coachman, come specially for me.

Exit BRANWELL, *euphoric*.

TABBY. He's like this lately – mad as a goat. Can I get you owt, doctor?

DOCTOR. I'm fine, Tabby. Is Anne about?

TABBY. She's in t'kitchen.

DOCTOR. Will you tell her I'm off soon.

Exit TABBY*; enter* TEACHER, *eating*.

TEACHER. How are you, doctor?

DOCTOR. Me? Like an old bird's nest.

TEACHER. You need a little bird to make you new again.

DOCTOR. Too true.

TEACHER. What a sad and momentous day this is, for Haworth. The loss of three intellectual giants in a single day. The doctor, teacher and curate, all gone at one stroke.

DOCTOR. I daresay Haworth will survive.

TEACHER. It's typically modest of you to say so, doctor. And perhaps a handful of ignorant townsfolk will agree. But men like ourselves are irreplaceable. Did I ever give you a copy of this? (*Offering his book*.)

DOCTOR (*declining it*). Two actually.

Enter ANNE.

TEACHER. Well, I mustn't get in your way. I've not said goodbye to Emily yet.

Exit TEACHER.

DOCTOR. He's the only one of us glad to be leaving. I'm dreading it. Are you sure you won't come, to help me look.

ANNE. If only I weren't so busy here... Charlotte told me there was some trouble last night. Between you and the curate. Is that true?

Pause.

DOCTOR. I've known you a long time, Anne. More than
twenty years. And you get more beautiful every day. If I
could, I'd marry you. There's just the one 'but' holding us
back. You try to hide it but it's there. You don't love me.

ANNE. Charlotte says that if you marry someone you respect,
then love can follow. But for now, it's true, you're a good
man and I'd like to say yes, sometimes I've tuned myself up
for it and thought I could say it, but I can't, it's hopeless. I'm
like a piano with its lid locked and the key missing.

Pause.

DOCTOR. I know you don't mean to hurt me. But the thought
of that the lost key is a torment. It's the curate, isn't it?

ANNE. What is?

DOCTOR. That's why you won't marry me. I'll murder him.

ANNE. It's nothing to do with William.

DOCTOR. What then? (*Pause.*) Say something.

ANNE. What can I say?

DOCTOR. Anything.

ANNE. I've said it all already.

Pause.

DOCTOR. You have. And I'm grateful. I'm not downcast. Far
from it. You know that chestnut tree in my garden. When I
looked at it this morning, I thought how restful it would be to
crawl under its branches and lie down. I could curl up next to
the trunk and fall asleep for ever. I'd be peaceful there, even
in winter with the wind shredding the leaves till there's
nothing left, only a skeleton. Yes, when I die, I'll die happy,
for having known you all these years.

ANNE. Don't talk of death.

DOCTOR. You're right. I shouldn't. Goodbye, my little seagull.
I really must go.

ANNE. I'll come out with you.

DOCTOR. No, you stay here. (*Walks away, then stops.*) Anne?

ANNE. What?

Pause.

DOCTOR. Will you tell Tabby to buy some coffee for when I get back? I've never liked tea.

Exit DOCTOR.

ANNE. I don't care what you say – I'm coming to see you off.

Exit ANNE. *Enter* CURATE *and* EMILY.

CURATE. All good things come to an end.

EMILY. We hoped you'd stay longer.

CURATE. Other parishes have more need of me than your father does.

EMILY. Anne will be distraught... We all will.

CURATE. I shall miss the place terribly. I feel so relaxed here – with you especially.

EMILY. Where's Anne? She'll want to see you before you go.

CURATE. You've all been so good to me.

EMILY. It's such a pity we never met your sister.

CURATE. She's not well. And I didn't like to trouble you.

EMILY. I'm sorry your time here hasn't been more rewarding.

CURATE. Oh, I've had my cross to bear. But life in general is getting better, you've got to admit – there's less suffering, less bloodshed, less injustice. In the old days, working people were treated like slaves. Now they've ideals, aspirations, notions of progress to drive them on. Everyone's working together to build the just city. And one day we'll succeed. Not now, perhaps, not soon, but it will come. When the workers are really educated, and those who're educated do real work.

EMILY. I hope you're right. (*Pause.*) Will you ever marry, do you think?

CURATE (*embarrassed*). I don't know. Why do you ask?

EMILY. The doctor would like to marry Anne. But so far she's refused him.

CURATE. I'm not surprised. He's a most aggressive and disagreeable man.

EMILY. Only because he's unhappy. Which he'd not be if Anne married him.

CURATE. Perhaps she should then.

EMILY. Do you really think so? Her affections seem to lie elsewhere these days. But she can't be sure whether they're reciprocated. Whether the loving words that have been spoken to her are the product of genuine feeling or mere whim. If only she knew where she stood.

CURATE. God makes all things clear in the fullness of time. I should get off.

EMILY. Wait, she's here.

Enter ANNE.

CURATE. I came to say goodbye.

ANNE. So did the doctor. He's just gone.

CURATE. Thank you for your kindness over these past months. I won't forget it. I won't forget you... Now, sadly, I have a train to catch.

ANNE. Can't you stay and have tea?

CURATE. I'd love to, but my sister's waiting.

ANNE. You should have brought her up here.

CURATE. Yes. I hope you won't think of me unkindly for not introducing you. And I'm sorry if... if my conduct towards you... if I've behaved in ways that might be misconstrued. But now I'm afraid I really must go.

Exit CURATE.

ANNE. What did he say to you?

EMILY. He said that life was getting better.

ANNE. For him, maybe.

EMILY. You know what he's like. Full of ideals. Never stops talking. Far too busy to think of marrying.

ANNE. He said that, did he?

EMILY. Not in so many words. But he's what he's always been – the lovesick curate. He'll never settle down.

ANNE. I suppose you're right.

EMILY. He doesn't look well, either.

ANNE. It's the weather. None of us do.

BRANWELL (*voice offstage*). You bitch, Charlotte, give it me now.

Enter a drunk and rowdy BRANWELL, carrying the wooden chest, and CHARLOTTE.

CHARLOTTE. How dare you speak to me like that!

BRANWELL. Shut your trap. Hand that key over.

CHARLOTTE. You're not having it. You've taken half the money already.

BRANWELL. Yes, and now I intend to put some money back.

CHARLOTTE. All you ever put in are IOUs.

BRANWELL. I'm warning you. Give me the key before I throttle you.

CHARLOTTE. If you want the key, you need Father's permission first.

BRANWELL. I have his permission. I'm his son and heir.

CHARLOTTE. There's hardly anything left in there.

BRANWELL. You'll not mind giving me the key, then.

EMILY. Give it him, Charlotte.

ANNE. Before he hurts you.

CHARLOTTE hands the key over.

BRANWELL. Thank you. (*Unlocks box, takes wad of money out.*) There, that should do me...

CHARLOTTE. To squander at the pub.

BRANWELL. I've just come back from the pub.

CHARLOTTE. We can see that.

BRANWELL. I've been drinking with Lydia's coachman, in fact. He brought me a message from her. You'll enjoy this, Charlotte. Mr Robinson changed his will before he died and added a clause preventing her from marrying me. Oh, she could marry me. But she'd lose everything if she did – the house, the land, the children, the inheritance. She still loves me, I know she does. But she hasn't the guts to stand up for me. All she wants is the life she knows. Dinner parties and roast duck and port and listening to idiots blathering about horses.

CHARLOTTE. You're well shot of her then.

BRANWELL. Oh, I knew you'd say that. But she's all I've loved these past years and now I've lost her.

Enter TABBY *with a book in her hand* – CHARLOTTE *and* ANNE *rush over to her, leaving* EMILY *alone with* BRANWELL.

Oh yes, that's it, go and fuss over Tabby, you think more of her than you do your own brother. No one in this family cares about me.

EMILY. I do.

BRANWELL. Well, you know why it's all over for me then. I've been felled, like a tree. My youth was a breeze but now a gale has brought me down.

Exit BRANWELL.

TABBY. He gets madder by the day, that one.

ANNE. Are you all right, Tabby? You look puffed out.

TABBY. I'm fit as five bullocks, miss. I've my own room, food, companionship, and work to keep me busy without killing me off. What more could a body ask? Only... Well, a couple of men from town are outside, see, and they gave me this book. You know I can't read but they say everyone's yapping about it and even strangers beyond Burnley are reading it. They asked if you'd write your name inside, because – excuse me, miss – they reckon it were you what wrote it.

CHARLOTTE. You mustn't listen to gossip, Tabby.

TABBY. There's nowt to it, then? I thought not. I'll tell them cheeky beggars where to stick their book.

CHARLOTTE. What did they say exactly?

TABBY. They say it's a book set on t'moors and there's a wicked villain in it and a servant who talks like I do and some right rough language an' all.

CHARLOTTE. Ah, *that* book, yes, there's some truth in what they're saying. But it's not my book... I have written one... But under another name... a man's name... in fact, there are three men... brothers... and they've each written a book... but the two other books are more, well, rough-hewn than my book... if you can call it mine. Sorry, this must sound very confusing, but I will explain it one day.

TABBY. Aye, miss, I hope you will.

CHARLOTTE. But I can't sign the book, obviously.

TABBY. Right, well, I'll give it back to 'em then.

    Exit TABBY.

ANNE. 'Rough-hewn': is that what you think?

CHARLOTTE. It wasn't a criticism.

ANNE. It sounded like one.

CHARLOTTE. You know how eccentric your punctuation is. And how morbid Emily's subject matter. But your books are very original. And I'm sure you'll go on to write even better ones.

ANNE. That's very encouraging, isn't it, Emily.

EMILY. I'm not going to write another book. I never wanted people talking about me.

CHARLOTTE. You can't stay invisible all your life.

EMILY. I could have, if you'd not mucked it up.

CHARLOTTE. You've had some good reviews.

EMILY. And bad ones.

CHARLOTTE. You put your whole being into that book.

EMILY. But I kept my name out of it. You'd no right to interfere.

CHARLOTTE. I was trying to help.

EMILY. You weren't helping me.

ANNE. Stop arguing – shhh.

Enter TEACHER, *who notices they're upset.*

TEACHER. No tears, please. It hurts to say goodbye to a trusted friend, I understand that. And on the whole I approve of passion – when teachers aren't passionate, children grow bored. But however deep your sorrow at my departure, I'd prefer you to control it.

Loud bang from outside.

What was that?

CHARLOTTE. Only Father. He does it every morning.

TEACHER. It's afternoon now.

ANNE. You've gone pale, Emily. What's the matter?

CHARLOTTE. She needs some food inside her. A wren would starve to death on what she eats.

ANNE. Are you feeling faint? What's up?

EMILY.
'We are as many as we were
That other night, when all were gay...
Yet is there something gone away...'

Awkward pause.

TEACHER. Yesterday I confiscated this face-mask from a boy at school. (*Puts it on.*) Do I look like a clown? (*Laughs.*) I do, don't I? The boys can be amusing sometimes, even if they don't know their ablatives.

ANNE. It suits you.

CHARLOTTE. It does – you really do look like a clown.

TEACHER. I'm a clown, everyone, a clown.

Enter PATRICK, *carrying a book.*

PATRICK. Who's that?

TEACHER. Only me.

PATRICK. Where's William?

CHARLOTTE. He's gone.

PATRICK. Without saying goodbye?

ANNE. You must have scared him off with your pistol.

PATRICK. I don't have my pistol.

CHARLOTTE. But we heard a bang.

ANNE. Something must have happened.

TEACHER. I'll go and see.

Exit TEACHER.

PATRICK. Did you realise, girls? Charlotte has written a book.

ANNE. We know.

PATRICK. I've been reading it. It's really quite good.

EMILY. Of course it's good.

ANNE. Emily and I have written books as well, Father.

EMILY. Shhh.

PATRICK. What's that?... Yes, it's really much better than you'd expect. I'm going to read some more.

Exit PATRICK.

ANNE. He has to know.

CHARLOTTE. And it's better he hears it from you.

ANNE. I've left my book on his desk.

CHARLOTTE. Good.

ANNE. And Emily's.

EMILY (*outraged*). Not mine as well.

ANNE. You saw how pleased he was for Charlotte. He'll be
    pleased for you too.

EMILY. I didn't write it to please people.

ANNE. Why did you then?

EMILY. Why does the wind blow? Because I had to.

CHARLOTTE. Don't you care what readers think?

EMILY. The book is what it is. I...

    Enter TEACHER.

CHARLOTTE. What is it?

TEACHER. I don't know how to say this.

CHARLOTTE. What?

TEACHER. Something terrible's happened.

ANNE. What?

CHARLOTTE. We'll come and help.

TEACHER. I don't know what caused it...

CHARLOTTE. Not the doctor.

ANNE. Not William.

EMILY. Not Branwell.

ANNE. I knew it.

CHARLOTTE. We heard the gun go off.

EMILY. He's shot himself. Hasn't he?

TEACHER. No one's been shot. It's not that.

CHARLOTTE. What then?

    Enter PATRICK *and* TABBY, *carrying* BRANWELL.

EMILY. What's happened?

PATRICK. He collapsed in the street.

CHARLOTTE. The drink again.

PATRICK. This is worse than drink.

TABBY. He were foaming at t'mouth.

PATRICK. A convulsion of some kind.

ANNE. Let me take him – he's too heavy, Tabby.

PATRICK. I'll take him. This is man's work. Boil some water, Tabby. You fetch the doctor, Mr Rand.

Exit TEACHER.

EMILY. How can we help?

PATRICK. You can't. We're in God's hands now. We must pray it's not as bad as it looks. That's all we can do.

ANNE. I'll come and sit with him.

PATRICK. I'm his father. I'll sit with him. Leave this to me.

Exit PATRICK.

EMILY. Whatever happens, we have to be brave. We've known suffering before. We're used to it.

CHARLOTTE. It's the waste I grieve for. The wreck of talent. He could have done anything.

EMILY. We mustn't despair. We have to go on.

ANNE. But if he dies… what will his life have been worth? What are *our* lives worth?

CHARLOTTE. You mustn't be frightened of death.

ANNE. I'm not frightened of death. If I knew I was dying, I think I could resign myself to it. Only… I long to do some good in the world before I leave it. I've all these schemes in my head and I'd hate them to come to nothing.

CHARLOTTE. Life's brief and bitter, I know. But there must be a purpose.

EMILY. There *is* a purpose. Think how we might have lived, just sitting there with our embroidery and the clock ticking. We've read, we've written, we've imagined, we've picked blackberries and wild flowers, we've walked the tops in sunshine and snow.

CHARLOTTE. And we've been happy. Not often, maybe, but once you've been happy, even briefly, it sustains you – whatever trials follow, whatever pains of sickness or shades of death, you can face them. Yes, we've suffered, but so have others. The huge mass of our fellow creatures have lives of hardship and privation. Why should we be favoured more than them?

ANNE. We'll work, we'll help Father, we'll keep writing poems and novels. And we'll look after each other. And my asthma will get better and Emily's cough will be cured.

CHARLOTTE. Soon the years will have passed and we'll be gone. Our faces will be forgotten, our voices will be forgotten, all that mattered to the three of us will be forgotten. But there'll be our books. And in the end, we *will* be remembered.

EMILY. Then we'll know what our purpose was.

ANNE. What we were born for.

CHARLOTTE. Yes, then we'll know. In the next life. Then we'll know.

The End.

A Nick Hern Book

We are Three Sisters first published in Great Britain as a paperback original in 2011 by Nick Hern Books, 14 Larden Road, London W3 7ST, in association with Northern Broadsides, Halifax

We are Three Sisters copyright © 2011 Blake Morrison

Blake Morrison has asserted his right to be identified as the author of this work

Cover photograph by Paul Floyd Blake / www.wonderassociates.com
Cover designed by Ned Hoste, 2H

Typeset by Nick Hern Books, London
Printed and bound by CPI Group (UK) Ltd, Croydon, CR0 4YY

A CIP catalogue record for this book is available from the British Library

ISBN   978 1 84842 214 8